Vatican City State

WORLD BIBLIOGRAPHICAL SERIES

General Editors:
Robert L. Collison (Editor-in-chief)
Sheila R. Herstein
Louis J. Reith
Hans H. Wellisch

VOLUMES IN THE SERIES

VOLUME 41

Vatican City State

Michael J. Walsh
Compiler

CLIO PRESS

OXFORD, ENGLAND · SANTA BARBARA, CALIFORNIA

British Library Cataloguing in Publication Data

Walsh, Michael J.
Vatican City State. – (World bibliographical series; v.41)
1. Vatican City – History – Bibliography
I. Title II. Series
016.945'634 DG800

ISBN 0-903450-72-0

Clio Press Ltd.,
Woodside House, Hinksey Hill,
Oxford OX1 5BE, England.
Providing the services of the European
Bibliographical Centre and the American
Bibliographical Center

American Bibliographical Center-Clio Press,
Riviera Campus, 2040 Alameda Padre Serra,
Santa Barbara, Ca. 93103, U.S.A.

Designed by Bernard Crossland
Computer typeset by Peter Peregrinus Ltd.
Printed in Great Britain
by Short Run Press Ltd., Exeter

THE WORLD BIBLIOGRAPHICAL SERIES

This series will eventually cover every country in the world, each in a separate volume comprising annotated entries on works dealing with its history, geography, economy and politics; and with its people, their culture, customs, religion and social organization. Attention will also be paid to current living conditions – housing, education, newspapers, clothing, etc. – that are all too often ignored in standard bibliographies; and to those particular aspects relevant to individual countries. Each volume seeks to achieve, by use of careful selectivity and critical assessment of the literature, an expression of the country and an appreciation of its nature and national aspirations, to guide the reader towards an understanding of its importance. The keynote of the series is to provide, in a uniform format, an interpretation of each country that will express its culture, its place in the world, and the qualities and background that make it unique.

SERIES EDITORS

Robert L. Collison (Editor-in-chief) is Professor Emeritus, Library and Information Studies, University of California, Los Angeles, and is currently the President of the Society of Indexers. Following the war, he served as Reference Librarian for the City of Westminster and later became Librarian to the BBC. During his fifty years as a professional librarian in England and the USA, he has written more than twenty works on bibliography, librarianship, indexing and related subjects.

Sheila R. Herstein is Reference Librarian and Library Instruction Coordinator at the City College of the City University of New York. She has extensive bibliographic experience and recently described her innovations in the field of bibliographic instruction in 'Team teaching and bibliographic instruction', *The Bookmark*, Autumn 1979. In addition, Doctor Herstein co-authored a basic annotated bibliography in history for Funk & Wagnalls *New encyclopedia*, and for several years reviewed books for *Library Journal*.

Louis J. Reith is librarian with the Franciscan Institute, St. Bonaventure University, New York. He received his PhD from Stanford University, California, and later studied at Eberhard-Karls-Universität, Tübingen. In addition to his activities as a librarian, Dr. Reith is a specialist on 16th century German history and the Reformation and has published many articles and papers in both German and English. He was also editor of the *American Society for Reformation Research Newsletter*.

Hans H. Wellisch is Associate Professor at the College of Library and Information Services, University of Maryland, and a member of the American Society of Indexers and the International Federation for Documentation. He is the author of numerous articles and several books on indexing and abstracting, and has most recently published *Indexing and abstracting: an international bibliography*. He also contributes frequently to *Journal of the American Society for Information Science, Library Quarterly*, and *The Indexer*.

75208

To
Clare

Contents

Contents

Preface

The Vatican City State is minute, and is entirely surrounded by the Republic of Italy. There is, therefore, little point in discussing its geography, and, though it may have a substantial garden, nothing has been written about its flora and fauna. In a country with only two buildings of any size — one a palace, the other a church — the category 'Town planning' hardly seems appropriate. The classification scheme common to the other volumes in this series does not fit. It has been instructive, however, to attempt to adapt the scheme to the Vatican's unique size and status. Considerable gaps have been revealed in what is available, especially in English, on topics such as the Vatican's educational system, or on its internal legal structure.

Despite these lacunae, the difficulty has been to know where to stop, what to leave out. Though the Vatican City has had so short a life it houses an institution which can reasonably claim to be among the oldest in the world. The departments which operate out of the tiny state affect the lives of hundreds of millions of Roman Catholics who regard the Vatican, with varying degrees of enthusiasm, as the headquarters of their religion.

But this book is not a bibliography of Catholicism, nor even of the papacy, though it has been impossible to avoid including some books about the former and a good many which directly or indirectly are concerned with the latter. This has also involved the inclusion of studies on the history of Rome, for the story of that city and the story of the papacy are inextricably linked. And the history of the papacy cannot be understood outside the history of Roman Catholicism, so a handful of general works on the history of the Church have been cited. Entries for the history of the Papal State, for the 'Roman Question' and for the papacy itself should need no explanation.

The heading 'Religion' may at first sight seem somewhat unnecessary, even if the *World Christian encyclopedia* foresees a doubling of the percentage of agnostics in the Vatican (to eight per cent) by the year 2000. Many Catholics would argue, however, that the Vatican exists simply to provide a home for those institutions whose purpose is to maintain the purity of Catholic faith and worship. So under the section on religion a number of works have been included which describe the faith that the Vatican claims to preserve and foster. Furthermore, in pursuance of this aim a great many speeches are made, statements issued and decrees passed. Care has been taken in the bibliography, either in the section on the papal office or following the entries for the various departments which administer the Church, to include the chief means whereby these decisions and so on are brought to the attention of the Catholic faithful.

It was remarked above that the Vatican has little scope for town planning. On the other hand the papacy has made an enormous impact upon the appearance of Rome as well as upon the buildings which go to make up the city state. Works about this particular aspect of papal patronage and endeavour have been listed under the heading of 'Environment', and this is taken to include artistic as well as architectural achievements. A small group of painters and architects have been given special attention because of the significance of their contribution to the fabric of the Vatican as it is today.

The most notable departure from the general practice of this series is in the section headed 'Literature'. The literary output of the Vatican City is exiguous, yet the city and the papacy have served as the background to, or the theme of, a number of novels and at least one play. A selection of these has been included, at least two of which (those by Peyrefitte) would in any case have been of importance for understanding the working of the Vatican. The present pope has written plays and poems, and his immediate predecessor published his collected essays; these and other examples are cited in the selection of post-war non-official papal writings.

The works included in this bibliography are mainly in English. I have always tried, however, to cite a major study no matter what the language — usually German or Italian — alongside the more readily accessible ones. Within the various sections entries have been grouped chronologically wherever this seemed appropriate, either in order of the period to which they refer, or in order of their own composition. Where such an arrangement did not seem suitable, books and articles of a more general nature, and more up-to-date studies, precede detailed works.

Users of this bibliography will undoubtedly notice a strong emphasis on the Middle Ages. Judged in terms of the authority it exercised over the peoples of the known world, the papacy as an institution was at the height of its power in the 13th century. I whole-heartedly endorse the opening words of Professor Barraclough's book, cited in this bibliography, that 'It is one of the great paradoxes of history that the papacy, as we think of it today, is in most essential ways a creation of medieval Europe'.

The compilation of this bibliography has been an unusually interesting and informative undertaking. I hope that those who use it will find it equally a pleasure to browse through and helpful to consult.

Introduction

It was the Emperor Augustus, ruler of the greater part of the known world when Christ was born, who divided the capital city of his empire into fourteen regions. Only one of the fourteen lay on the right, or west, bank of the River Tiber. It was called the Vaticanum, and its most distinctive feature was a hill, together with a valley and a plain.

The Vatican hill is not one of the seven upon which, traditionally, Rome is said to have been built. It would be more accurate to say that it was from the Vatican that Rome was built because the area was then, and still is, valued for its brickyards. Its wine, on the other hand, was bitter and the air was thought to be unhealthy. Nero's gardens were there, and so was the circus where many Christians were martyred, and from which the obelisk came that today stands in St. Peter's Square. There was a race course, a stadium for water sports, a sanctuary to a pagan goddess, and the great tomb of the Emperor Hadrian. In the year 330 the Emperor Constantine had part of the hill levelled to make way for a church to be constructed around a monument which had itself been built over a pauper's grave.

The grave was thought to be that of Peter, the apostle whose personality emerges most vividly from the pages of the New Testament. Apart from one ambiguous remark, however, there is no evidence in the New Testament that Peter visited Rome, and whether he did so or not used to be a matter of acrimonious debate between Roman Catholic apologists and their adversaries. Nowadays the point is almost universally conceded, and discussion, so far as there is any, has shifted away from the fact to the significance of the fact, something which is not relevant here. It is not in dispute that from the earliest years of the Christian era Peter was believed to have been the leader of the Christians in Rome and to have died a martyr's death there, probably in the year AD 67. In modern terms he might be called the bishop of Rome, though, as any of the histories listed in the bibliography which follows will make clear, that term has to be used with caution.

The origins of the Vatican City State have to be traced back to the office of the bishop of Rome, not to the geographical area the city state now occupies. The significance of the Vatican to the Christians of Rome was as a shrine, not as the residence of their bishop. At first it would seem the bishop had no fixed place to live. Constantine gave him

Introduction

the former imperial palace of the Lateran. A nearby barracks of a rebellious cavalry regiment was pulled down to make way for a church. The Lateran basilica was, and still is, the cathedral church of Rome. It was the Lateran which gave its name to the treaty between the bishop of Rome and the Kingdom of Italy that set up the Vatican City State in 1929.

The States of the Church

At the same time as he was ordering the construction in Rome of a shrine to honour St. Peter, Constantine was giving instructions for the building of a new imperial capital in the east upon the site of the old Greek city of Byzantium. It was to carry the emperor's own name: Constantinople. It rapidly became the most important city of the empire, and even when there was an emperor living in the west he resided in Milan or Ravenna rather than in Rome. Rome's bishop increasingly came to play the part of protector of the city. Nothing symbolized this new role more dramatically than the confrontation in 452 between Bishop Leo and Attila the Hun when the bishop dissuaded the barbarian leader from laying siege to the city. A later bishop, Gregory the Great at the end of the 6th century, found himself paying the troops supposedly sent by the emperor in the east to guard the city from the latest group of barbarians, the Lombards. Gregory also had to find the money to buy food not just for the inhabitants of Rome but for the thousands of refugees who had fled there.

That he was able to do so was the result not only of good financial management but also of his efforts to reorganize the estates in and around Rome – and far beyond – which had come, one way or another, into the possession of the Church. The revenues of the estates had been intended for the upkeep of the shrines of the city, above all for the shrine of St. Peter, but Gregory had to use it for the welfare of the city's inhabitants and the armies sent to defend them. In the end the imperial troops proved insufficient. The king of the Franks was called upon to help. King Pepin reconquered from the Lombards the lands which had once belonged to the imperial duchies of Ravenna and Rome, and handed them back to the bishop of the latter city. It is this 'donation of Pepin' which is generally taken to mark the beginning of the States of the Church. It was in 756.

The States of the Church were, and still are, more commonly known as the Papal States. The bishops of Rome claimed a right to the exclusive use of the title 'pope' from the 11th century onwards, though in earlier centuries it had been more generally used of bishops, and it is still used of the Coptic Patriarch of Alexandria. It means no more than 'father', and in that quite ordinary sense it is used by Greek parish clergy to this day. In its more formal sense it is usually taken as the title of the bishop of Rome in his office of head (on earth, a Roman Catholic would hasten to add) of the 700 million and more Roman Catholics throughout the world. Popes will sign themselves as such, but the title occurs nowhere in the list contained in the Vatican's official yearbook, the *Annuario Pontificio*. The most important title of any pope is 'bishop of Rome'. It is to that office he is elected. The other offices and titles, including that of 'sovereign of the Vatican City State', follow automatically upon election. Few are commonly used except, in its adjectival form, 'pontifex maximus'. Originally this was the title for the chief priest of pagan Rome, and eventually it was taken over by the emperors. When they ceased to use it the bishops of Rome adopted it with the result that 'pontiff' or, more usually, 'pontifical' are synonymous with 'pope' or 'papal' respectively.

The bishops of Rome had long claimed, and to some degree exercised, jurisdiction over an area wider than Rome and its environs. Their involvement with the Frankish empire gave their assertion of an authority co-extensive with − at least − western Christianity some credibility. Without the Franks they could hardly have exercised their authority over the Papal States, and often enough conflicts with the Roman nobility limited the amount of control they could hope for even in that city. The development of the feudal system, therefore, was a distinct benefit to the popes. That structure of authority could contain within itself a wide variety of forms of local government, allied with an ultimate suzerainty invested in the person of the pope. It was actively promoted by a number of pontiffs including Adrian IV, the − so far − only English pope. At the beginning of the 13th century Innocent III established an effective machinery of government, later popes set up provincial taxation offices, and offices for the administration of justice. By the middle of the century there were a number of local 'parliaments' and the always very variable territorial extent of the states had been notably increased.

But then, in the 14th century, came the prolonged 'exile' of the popes at Avignon, part of the Papal States from the middle of that century. The absence of the bishop from Italy allowed a good deal of independence to grow among local magnates, and the efforts, at first highly successful, of Cardinal Albornoz to counteract such movements were themselves brought to nothing by the schism which followed the return from Avignon. During it there were two, and sometimes three, men claiming with some reason to be the lawful bishop of Rome. By

Introduction

the time Martin IV was elected in 1417 to put an end to the schism, the papacy had forfeited much of its international authority, but at least Martin was able to begin, and begin successfully, a sustained attempt to win back control of the Papal States. The magnates who governed them proved either too weak or too divided to resist Roman centralization. In particular, they proved incapable of resisting the challenge presented, on behalf of the bishop of Rome, by Cesare Borgia, the highly talented son of Pope Alexander VI, whom Machiavelli took as his model when writing *The Prince.* Alexander may have intended to endow his own family with the territories over which control had been regained for the papacy, but the circumstances of his death, coupled with Cesare's own sickness at a crucial moment, prevented this happening. The states remained in papal hands. The popes were to need every penny of revenue from their territories to finance the enormous expansion of the papal court, and the papal patronage of the arts, in the course of the 16th century.

The popes and their capital

The presence in Rome of the shrines of the Apostles Peter and Paul, and the importance of the bishop of the city, could not fail to have an impact upon the town from the very earliest times, whether in terms of churches, administrative buildings (sometimes themselves churches), monasteries, residences for pilgrims and so on. It affected the names of streets, piazzas, even of whole areas – the Borgo, for example, is derived from the English 'borough', and marks the residence of Anglo-Saxon pilgrims. Papal influence went further. Papal ideology was given visible expression in the decoration, or even the shape, of buildings. Two examples will be enough to illustrate the point, for it is something touched upon by several of the items in the bibliography. In the church of Santa Maria Maggiore the mosaic decoration on the triumphal arch, completed in the 430s, skilfully employed imperial iconography to suggest that the Church had now replaced the emperor as the protector of the city. In the second instance, a 13th-century chapel was decorated with scenes depicting the legendary 'Donation of Constantine', upon which much of the papal claim to temporal as well as to spiritual authority rested.

But it was the papacy of the Renaissance which made most impact upon the city of Rome. Pope Julius II began the destruction of the basilica which Constantine had ordered to be built over the shrine of Peter. Julius envisaged it as the setting for his own tomb, and laid the

Introduction

foundation stone of the new St. Peter's in April 1506. But it was not for another 120 years that the basilica could be consecrated. In between times it had provided employment for Bramante, Michelangelo, Bernini, and a whole host of other lesser-known architects, painters and craftsmen. Meanwhile the Vatican Palace, basically a 15th-century building as it now survives, and the papal residence in Rome from the return from Avignon, was decorated by Raphael and his disciples, along with many others. Those artists mentioned above by name have been given special prominence in this book. Had it been an exhaustive bibliography room would have had to be found for many, many more. The famous Sistine Chapel, for instance, where popes are elected and where tourists gaze at Michaelangelo's paintings on the ceiling and, particularly, at the 'Last Judgement' behind the altar, was constructed by Sixtus IV, whose name it bears, between 1475 and 1483. Though it is the work of Michelangelo which claims attention, Botticelli, Pintoricchio, Ghirlandaio and many others worked upon it before him.

Sixtus IV also added considerably to the Vatican Library, though its foundation in its present form is usually attributed to the earlier Nicholas V. The buildings to house the collection, however, were started by another Sixtus, Sixtus V, at the end of the 16th century. All this patronage required cash. Sixtus V brought order back to the Papal States by draconian measures, and his financial reforms increased the flow of money into the papal treasury. But in the end the demands were too great. The costs of the papal court and its appendages were a constant drain upon the resources of the states. They went into economic decline. Moreover, the system of government, a model of its kind when Cesare Borgia instituted it, was outmoded by the time of the French Revolution. The armies of Napoleon were not unwelcome to many within the states, which were annexed to France in 1810.

The Roman Question

It was not self-evident to the Great Powers that, after the fall of Napoleon and the collapse of his empire, the Papal States should be restored to the control of the papacy. Yet they were eventually given back in their entirety, except for the areas — including Avignon — which lay within the borders of France. It was a triumph for papal diplomacy, but it was far from welcome to many of the intellectual laity in the states who had hoped to play a greater part in government. Their hopes were not easily to be brushed aside. There was a revolt in 1831, followed by reforms which proved insufficient. Pius IX, elected pope in 1846,

Introduction

seemed at first to promise great things, but once again aspirations were disappointed when he refused to head a coalition of Italian states against Austrian pretensions in the peninsula. In 1848 the pope had to flee Rome. He was offered asylum by Queen Victoria and was restored by the combined efforts of France and Austria. In 1859 several of the provinces of the Papal States revolted and sought unity with the Kingdom of Piedmont. By 1861 the Papal States, once some 5,000 square miles of Italian territory, were limited to the city of Rome and its environs, and the city itself was proclaimed the capital of the Kingdom of Italy. The proclamation was a little precipitate. Rome was secure for the pope while French troops continued to guard it. In 1870 they were withdrawn. After only a token resistance by papal forces Italian troops marched into the city and annexed it. The pope became 'the prisoner in the Vatican'.

That was largely his own doing. With the fall of the city the 'Roman Question', as far as the Great Powers were concerned, was at an end. For the papacy it was, in a way, just beginning. In 1871 the government of Italy passed the Law of Guarantees. The extraterritoriality of the Vatican, of the Lateran and of Castel Gandolfo, the papal summer residence, was recognized. The pope was to be given the honours of a head of state, conceded diplomatic privileges, allowed to retain some armed forces, granted immunity from Italian law, and given an annual allowance of 3 million lire. He was, however, to renounce any claim to temporal sovereignty. Pius IX rejected an accommodation.

The Vatican City's constitution

It was an agreement very similar to the Law of Guarantees which was reached in 1929 to end the 'Roman Question' to papal satisfaction. But there was no continuity in international law between the Papal States, which ceased to exist in 1870, and the Vatican City State which came into being sixty years later. It is not because of a direct link that so much about the Papal States has been included in this bibliography. The issue is a different one, and more concerned with the papacy than with the Papal States. The form which the papacy has taken has developed over the centuries, but popes from the 4th to the 19th centuries were never without some form of 'power base' which was — and, indeed, still is — different in kind from that enjoyed by any other spiritual leader except, at one time perhaps, the Dalai Lama. The papal court, and the machinery of government which surrounds the pope, was constructed in a very different environment from the one within which it now operates. If, by some terrible accident, the whole of the Vatican City, and the whole of Rome itself – for very few of the offices which go to make up the central government of the Catholic Church operate out of the Vatican City properly so-called – were suddenly blotted out and the machinery had to be reassembled from nothing, it is very doubtful if the outcome would much resemble the Roman Curia as it is today. That is a personal view perhaps, but it is undoubtedly true that the Roman Curia as it now exists is a product of the lengthy development of the papacy as a spiritual institution and of the Papal States as a temporal one. As it was set up in 1929 the Vatican City State's purpose is to provide the papacy and the Roman Curia with a geographical base from which to exercise authority over the whole Roman Catholic Church. The shape of the papacy, of the court which serves it, of the offices which constitute it, even the titles borne by its functionaries, reflect a history which is far longer than the history of the Vatican City State.

The Vatican City's legal status

The point has to be made firmly, for it would seem to follow from this that the Vatican City is not, as it is usually presented, a sovereign entity. It came into being for no other purpose than to provide a territorial base for the pope and his Curia. Collectively, the pope and Curia are known as the Holy See – a somewhat misleading term, since in all other similar contexts 'see' means diocese. The Holy See is, and has long been, recognized in international law as itself a sovereign entity. It did not cease to exist when the Papal States finally fell in 1870. Many nations retained or, as in the case of the United Kingdom, established diplomatic relations with the Holy See after the Italians annexed Rome as their capital city and before the Lateran Treaty set up the Vatican City State. And as the opening words of the Lateran Treaty make clear, it was with the Holy See that the government of Italy was negotiating to bring the Vatican City into being. In a phrase which reveals much about the way in which Vatican officialdom thinks of itself, one of the pope's most distinguished diplomatic representatives has written that 'The Holy See is to the Church what the government is to the state' (H. E. Cardinale, *The Holy See and the international order*, p. 85). It is perhaps even more interesting to ask about the relationship between the Holy See and the Vatican City. The latter in effect exists solely to serve the purposes of the former. It has no other *raison d'être*. Since no one is disposed nowadays to deny the sovereignty, whether territorially

Introduction

grounded or not, of the Holy See, the Vatican City would seem to be not itself a sovereign entity but a vassal state of the Holy See.

These issues of sovereignty may seem academic, but the independence of the Vatican is increasingly a matter of debate in Italy as a consequence of recent financial scandals involving the Vatican Bank, known officially as the 'Institute for the Works of Religion' or, from the initials of its name in Italian, as the IOR. In practice it has been the Concordat, agreed at the same time as the Lateran Treaty, which has presented most problems in the relationship between the Vatican and the Italian state. The head of this apparently sovereign state is not only bishop of Rome. He is also primate, or senior bishop, of Italy. While the pope was an Italian – and only Italians had been elected since the death of the Dutch Adrian VI in 1523 – the confusion was all the greater. The choice of a Polish cardinal in 1978 has meant a distancing of the Holy See from the internal affairs of Italy, but the position still remains ambiguous.

Administrative organization

Vatican City

The Vatican City is, then, a mass of peculiarities. The most obvious of them is its size. It is not simply the smallest country in the world, it is only a third of the area of Monaco which comes next in order of minuteness. The Vatican City proper comprises just under 109 acres, roughly a third of which is covered with buildings, a third with pavement, and a third with gardens. Papal territory outside the city is bigger than the city itself, and amounts to a further 160 acres. The pope rules over this miniscule area as an absolute sovereign, both spiritual and temporal. In theory at least, he probably has greater power than any other individual, or parliament, in the world. He has, however, very few people over whom to exercise it. In November 1980 the wife of a member of the Swiss Guard gave birth to a daughter. The child became the 352nd citizen of the city state, and only the 14th person to be born there since its creation in 1929. The family had Vatican citizenship because they were authorized to live within its boundaries. Once that authorization ceases, anyone holding Vatican citizenship reverts to being a citizen of their previous country of birth or adoption. There is a form of safety-net allowed for in the Lateran Treaty, whereby anyone who would be rendered stateless by loss of Vatican citizenship automatically acquires that of Italy. Cardinals who are permanently attached to the Curia, papal representatives around the world (who are, incident-

Introduction

ally, emissaries of the Holy See and not of the Vatican City), and some full-time employees such as members of the Swiss Guard, are Vatican citizens. But this is a status not given to everyone who works within the city, nor even to all who reside there.

The territory is owned by the pope of the time as a kind of personal possession. No one else, for example, can acquire land in the city. The fact is neatly symbolized by the fact that the Vatican flag is the papal flag, a banner divided vertically into two equal parts of yellow — nearer the pole — and white. The white is emblazoned with crossed keys surmounted by the papal tiara or triple crown. The same tiara and crossed keys, set against a red background, constitute the Vatican's coat of arms, but each pope has his own escutcheon. The Vatican City also has the right to its own stamps and coinage. Both are used — especially the former — but they are collectors' items as well, and a means of producing revenue.

The Vatican City is technically part of the diocese of Rome, but the pope's spiritual responsibility for those who live within it, and within the other extraterritorial possessions, is exercised by a special vicar general. The pope's authority over the Vatican City as its head of state is delegated to a commission of cardinals, presided over by the cardinal secretary of state. In theory there are also a governor and a general councillor, but both positions are, and have long been, vacant. The Cardinatial Commission has been the official governing body of the state since 1969. As laid out in the *Annuario Pontificio* at the beginning of 1982, the administration of the Vatican City State is as follows:

Pontifical Commision for the Vatican City State, consisting of a number of cardinals presided over by the cardinal secretary of state.

Council of State, consisting entirely of lay people, and presided over by the layman who is the state's chief executive.

Administration, with the following departments: General Secretariat; Legal Department; Personnel; Accounts; Philatelic and Numismatic Bureau; Department of Posts and Telegraphs; Department of Trade; Central Security; Information Office for tourists and pilgrims.

Directorate General of Papal Monuments, Museums and Galleries. There have been papal collections of art open to the public at least since the 16th century.

Directorate General of Technical Services.

Directorate General of Vatican Radio, which is run by Jesuits.

Introduction

Directorate General of Health Services. Dependent on it is the pharma-
ceutical department.

Directorate of the Vatican Observatory, which is also run by Jesuits,
and is housed at Castel Gandolfo.

Directorate of Archaeological Research.

Directorate of Papal Villas.

Courts, before which are brought a small number of civil, and a rather
larger number of criminal (largely traffic) offences each year.
Composed of: the judge; Court of First Instance; Court of Appeal;
Court of Cessation, to consider defects in procedure.

Health and Welfare Fund, set up in 1953 for those working in the
Vatican City.

Permanent Commission for the Protection of the Historical Monuments
of the Holy See, which was first set up in 1923, but assumed
wider responsibilities after the Lateran Treaty.

Palatine Administration

The pope has responsibility for some departments of the Vatican in his
role as bishop of Rome, rather than as leader of the Catholic Church
world-wide. These are grouped together under the heading of the Palatine Administration. They are not part of the government of the whole
Church, nor are they directly part of the administration of the Vatican
City as such. Again in the order laid down in the *Annuario Pontificio*
they are:

Reverend Fabric of St. Peter's, which dates from the rebuilding of the
basilica during the 16th century. This department has responsibility for the building itself, and has on its staff lawyers, architects
and technical experts.

Apostolic Vatican Library, the origins of which lie in the 4th century,
and there was a cardinal librarian in the 8th century. Attached to
it is the Vatican School of Library Science.

Secret Archives of the Vatican, which are, for the most part, secret no
longer. Attached to it is the Vatican School of Palaeography,
Diplomatic and Archive Studies, which was founded in 1884.

Vatican Polyglott Press, which was started in 1587 to print bibles, and
which, in 1908, merged with the Polyglott Press begun in 1626 to
serve the Congregation of Propaganda.

Introduction

Vatican Publishing House, independent of the Polyglott Press only since 1926.

L'Osservatore Romano, the Vatican daily paper, which began life as an independent publication in 1861, but was purchased by Leo XIII in 1890. The weekly edition in English began in 1968. There are also weekly editions in French, Spanish, Portuguese and German, as well as a monthly edition in Polish which began in 1980.

Pontifical Administration of the Patriarchal Basilica of St. Paul. The Lateran Treaty transferred St. Paul's Outside the Walls to the papacy, and a special administration was established to look after the basilica and its immediate surroundings.

College of Cardinals

When 'the Vatican' is referred to, it is rarely the city state which is meant, and scarcely at all the Palatine Administration. The term is used loosely to indicate the central administration of the Roman Catholic Church, the Roman Curia. 'Curia' simply means court, though not in the common, even if derivative, sense of legal tribunal. It means court in the original sense of a collective name for those surrounding a monarch or other head of state, and refers to those departments – dicasteries is the preferred term – which govern every aspect of the life of the Church. The older, and the more important, of these dicasteries are called Congregations, though because this is the Vatican 'Sacred' is tacked on to the front of each name (it is left out here for brevity's sake). A prefect heads each Congregation. The post is always held by a cardinal.

From the earliest times the leader of the Christians in Rome must have had helpers and advisers. In the 4th century one group emerged as an identifiable entity: the Apostolic Chancery, still in existence to handle papal correspondence. For the most part those who helped the bishop were drawn from among the Roman clergy. Among his chief advisers were the bishops from the dioceses around Rome, the seven suburbicarian sees. He was also served by the priests who worked in the major churches of the city, and by the deacons who looked after the welfare of the city's inhabitants. As Kuttner explains in the article cited later in the bibliography, this group of important clerics, bishops, priests and deacons of Rome became known as cardinals. In the 11th century the 'college', as the group was collectively known, became the pope's chief counsellors when gathered together in a consistory. The right of electing a pope was made exclusively theirs in the 12th century. In the following century the present 'conclave' system came into being

Introduction

in an attempt to speed up elections by locking the cardinals in until they had reached agreement. They have usually chosen one of themselves, especially in recent centuries, but there is no rule which says they must do so. The 'Curial' cardinals reside in Rome to run the ecclesiastical machine, but the title is also bestowed on important prelates who have pastoral responsibilities around the world − the archbishops of New York and of Westminster, for example, would normally be 'given the red hat' − a reference to the colour of their formal dress, Catholic prelates being conveniently colour-coded. To maintain the fiction that the pope is chosen by the Roman clergy, each cardinal, no matter where he is based, has some honorary, or 'titular', responsibility in Rome. All of them, unless excused on grounds of health or of age, will regularly travel to Rome to sit upon the central bodies of the various Congregations.

Up until the 16th century the cardinals as a college, albeit at times a very divided one, were able to exercise considerable power. In 1588, however, Sixtus V reformed the Curia. He broke it up into a number of individual departments much as it is today, and this also broke the power of the cardinals as a group. The consistory became a formal, ceremonial gathering to ratify papal decisions, though the present pope has given some indication that he might wish to revive it as a consultative body. The Congregations over which the cardinals preside have passed through a whole series of reforms, and changes of title, since they first began. In what follows it will soon become clear that there was a major shake-up under Pope Paul VI in 1967.

Roman Curia

The Congregations and other offices of the Curia are listed below for the most part in the order in which they appear in the *Annuario.*

Secretariat of State. In the 16th century popes came to choose their chief adviser from within their own family: hence the development of the office of 'cardinal nephew'. By the end of the 17th century, however, the secretary of state, an office first instituted in 1644, had entirely replaced the cardinal nephew. Since 1967 the secretariat has been concerned with the Church's overall government, and with oversight of the other departments of the Curia. It is divided into the following: the Cipher Office; the Chancery for Apostolic Briefs (letters); relations between the Congregations; correspondence section; relations with international organizations; information and documentation; honours and ceremonial; administration; general services. The secretariat is also responsible for the publication of the *Acta Apostolicae Sedis.* Dependent upon it is the Central Statistical Office, set up in 1967. This office publishes the *Annuarium Statisticum Ecclesiae* and the *Annuario Pontificio.* The latter, however, has been in existence since the early years of the 18th century. Under its present name it dates back to 1912. The secretariat also includes permanent commissions for personnel, for promotion within the Curia, and for honours.

Council for the Public Affairs of the Church was originally a separate Congregation, then became part of the Secretariat of State. It was made independent of the secretariat, and given its present title, in 1967. It is headed by the secretary of state and is the Vatican's department for foreign affairs. It includes the Pontifical Commission for Russia, which began in 1930 and has oversight of Latin-rite Catholics inside Russia.

Congregation for the Doctrine of the Faith was founded as the 'Universal Inquisition' in 1542, and was renamed the Holy Office in 1908. Its original function was to prosecute heresy, and it still retains that role, though when Paul VI changed its name once more in 1965 he gave it the new task of promoting orthodoxy as well as condemning error. Under its aegis operate the International Theological Commission, founded 1969, and the Pontifical Biblical Commission, founded 1902.

Congregation for Bishops can claim to go back to 1588, but with its present name and function it has been in existence only since 1967. It has oversight of diocesan affairs, and the appointment of bishops, in all parts of the world other than those which fall within the competence of the Congregations for Eastern Churches and for the Evangelization of Peoples (see below). It includes the Permanent Commission for Latin America, instituted in 1958 to study Latin American affairs, and to link the Curia to that part of the world; the General Council for Latin America, instituted in 1963 to link the above with European and North American organizations which have an interest in Latin America, and divided into two sections, the first studying aid with personnel, the second financial assistance; the Pontifical Commission for the Apostolate among Migrants and Tourists. This was founded in 1970 and publishes *On the Move.*

Congregation for Eastern Churches. When it was founded in 1862 it was part of the Congregation de Propaganda Fide (see below), but has

Introduction

been independent since 1917. Its main area of responsibility is the Middle East, but includes Afghanistan. Dependent on it are the Special Commission for the Liturgy and the Pontifical Mission for Palestine.

Congregation for the Sacraments and Divine Worship. The two Congregations which merged in 1975 to produce this one can still be distinguished in the two departments into which it is divided, the first for the sacraments, the second for divine worship. Dependent on it are the Special Commission on Holy Orders (concerned with priests who wish to return to the lay state), and the Special Commission on Non-Consummated Marriages. The Congregation publishes *Notitiae*.

Congregation for the Clergy. In its present form, this has existed only since 1967. It has three departments, the duties of the first being to foster the spiritual and intellectual life of the clergy — under which there is a special commission on the geographical distribution of priests; of the second to foster the apostolate, especially catechetics; and of the third to oversee the administration of the Church's property — and pensions.

Congregation for Religious and for Secular Institutes. Originally established in 1586 as a channel for communication with the religious orders, this Congregation was then linked to that of Bishops. It separated again in 1908, and was later given responsibility for secular institutes when these arrived on the scene. There are now two departments, one for religious and one for secular institutes, and the present name was given in 1967 to cover both. Under this Congregation comes the council for the relations between the Congregation and the International Union of Superiors General.

Congregation for the Evangelization of Peoples. This Congregation began in the 16th century but was revived in 1622 with the title 'De Propaganda Fide' (for the propagation of the faith) which still remains as an appendage to the latest version of the name. It oversees work in missionary territories, and includes: Laboratory for the Restoration of Archives; Commission for Theology, Spirituality and Missionary Zeal; Review Commission (for all groups and organizations linked to the Congregation); Commission for the Study of the Apostolate; Commission for Catechetics and Catechists; Supreme Committee (of the agencies listed below); Superior Council (of the agencies listed below); General Secretariat of the Pontifical Missionary Work for the Propagation of the Faith; General Secretariat for the Pontifical Work of St. Peter the Apostle; General Secretariat for the Work of the Holy Infancy; General Secretariat of the Pontifical Missionary Union; International Centre for Missionary Zeal. The Congregation publishes *Annuario, Bibliografia Missionaria, Acta Pontificalium Operum, Le Pontificie Cooperazione Missionarie e Solidarietà tra le Chiese, Aspetti Pastorali delle Pontificie Opere Missionarie, Status Seminariorum Indigenorum, Documents-Omnis Terrae* (in French, English and Spanish), and *Agenzia Internationale Fides* (in the above languages but including Italian and German).

Congregation for the Causes of Saints was set up in 1588 as part of the Congregation of Rites, but given independent existence in 1969. Includes the Department of the Promoter General of the Faith and the Department of History and Hagiography.

Congregation for Catholic Education. This Congregation was set up in 1588 to supervise the University of Rome which, as the 'Sapienza', was the chief university of the Papal States until the fall of Rome. It also had responsibility for the other major Italian universities. It became the Congregation for Studies, and then of Universities and Seminaries. It took its present form in 1967, and oversees pontifical work for priestly vocations. The Congregation publishes *Seminarium*.

Tribunals

Apostolic Penitentiary. This dates back to the 13th century. It is now concerned with moral matters which are reserved to the Holy See to decide upon.

Supreme Tribunal of the Signatura Apostolica. It was the duty of this office, existing in a stable form from the 15th century, to pass for papal signing replies to requests for justice or for favours. By the end of the same century it had itself become a court. It is now the highest court within the Curia, and has jurisdiction over all administrative decisions in the Church.

Roman Rota. When first established — by the 15th century at least — the Rota was a general court. It is now mainly concerned with marriage cases, and includes the Rota Seminar, for the training of judges and advocates. The Rota publishes *Decisiones seu Sententiae*.

Introduction

Secretariats

Secretariat for Christian Unity. First set up in 1960. The Commission for Religious Relations with Judaism, established in 1974, is separate from, but linked to, the secretariat. The secretariat publishes *Information Service* (in Italian, French and English).

Secretariat for Non-Christians. Established 1964. The Commission for Religious Relations with Islam was also set up in 1974 as separate from, but linked to, the secretariat. The secretariat publishes a *Bulletin* (in Italian, French and English).

Secretariat for Non-Believers. Established in 1965, it publishes *Ateismo e Dialogo* (in Italian, French, English and Spanish).

Councils, commissions and committees

Pontifical Council for the Laity began provisionally in 1967 and was given firm status in 1976. Its brief is the role of the laity in the Church's apostolate. It publishes *Laity Today* in French, English and Spanish and *Information Service* and *Documentation Service* in the same languages plus Italian and German.

Pontifical Commission 'Justice and Peace' began provisionally in 1967 and was given firm status in 1976. It studies questions concerning justice and peace, development and the rights of man and other topics both to deepen the Church's teaching on social issues, and to make that teaching more widely known.

Pontifical Commission for the Revision of the Code of Canon Law. Established in 1963 to perform the function accurately described in the title. It publishes *Communicationes.*

Pontifical Commission for the Revision of the Code of Oriental Canon Law is a successor, set up in 1972, of a commission originally established in 1935 to produce a code of law for the eastern Churches in communion with Rome. It also prepares definitive texts of the sources of that law, texts which are of considerable importance historically as well as legally. It publishes *Nuntia.*

Pontifical Commission for the Interpretation of the Decrees of the Second Vatican Council.

Pontifical Commission for Social Communication began in 1948 as a 'watchdog' body concerned with the cinema. From 1954 it extended its interests — officially — to radio and television. Ten years later newspapers and periodicals were added to its brief, and it was given its present name. It has charge of the Press Office of the Holy See, and the Vatican Film Library, which began in 1959 for the purpose of collecting films and television recordings concerning the life of the Church. It publishes annually the *Bulletin de la C.P.C.S.* and a daily *Bolletino – Sala Stampa della S. Sede* (basically a press release).

Pontifical Council Cor Unum, a co-ordinating agency, set up in 1971, for developing countries and charitable organizations which send funds. It also dispenses charity on behalf of the pope.

Pontifical Council for the Family. A committee concerned with the pastoral care of families was set up in 1973, and it became a 'council' in 1981.

Council of Cardinals for the Study of the Organizational and Economic Problems of the Holy See.

Pontifical Abbacy of St. Jerome for the Revision and Emendation of the Vulgate. The Vulgate is the Latin edition of the Bible produced in the 4th century by St. Jerome. The purpose of the abbacy, which in 1933 replaced the original commission revising the Vulgate, is to establish the basic text as far as is possible. The abbacy belongs to the Benedictine Congregation of Solesme.

Pontifical Commission for Sacred Archaeology was founded in 1852 for the care and preservation of the ancient cemeteries and other monuments of early Christianity. It now has authority over all catacombs in Italy, regulating access to them, publishing papers about them and so on.

Pontifical Committee of Historical Sciences. The original 'Cardinatial Commission for the Study of History' began in 1883. The present name was adopted in 1954.

Pontifical Commission for the Ecclesiastical Archives of Italy. This commission, which started in 1955, became fully fledged in 1960. It aims to assist bishops and other ecclesiastical superiors who have responsibility for archives.

Central Pontifical Commission for Sacred Art in Italy. Since 1924 the scope of this commission has been to preserve and improve the Church's 'artistic patrimony' in Italy. It is also consulted about the constructing of new ecclesiastical buildings, and co-operates closely with Italian government agencies.

Introduction

Cardinatial Commission for the Pontifical Sanctuaries of Pompeii, Loreto and Bari. Leo XIII set up a commission to care for the shrine at Pompeii. Paul VI added Loreto to it in 1965, and John Paul II added Bari in 1980.

Offices

Apostolic Chamber is one of the Vatican's oldest offices, dating back to the 11th century. It has the task of administering the Holy See's possessions during a *sede vacante* (i.e., between the death of one pope and the election of the next), and is presided over by the cardinal camerlengo (chamberlain) or the vice-camerlengo.

Prefecture for the Economic Affairs of the Holy See was founded in 1967 to oversee and co-ordinate all the Holy See's economic activities. Responsibility is shared among three cardinals.

Administration of the Patrimony of the Apostolic See was set up in its present form only in 1967 but has roots much further back. It is the Vatican's 'central bank' as far as international financial institutions are concerned, and it has to find the greater part – though not all – of the running expenses of the pope and Curia. It is divided into two sections: Ordinary Section, which administers all the patrimony of the Holy See except that which is controlled by the Extraordinary Section, set up to administer the funds which came to the Holy See as a consequence of the Lateran Treaty.

Prefecture of the Pontifical Household was instituted in 1967, though its present name was given to it the following year. It has responsibility for papal audiences and for the papal apartments, for ceremonies (other than religious ones) and questions of precedence. Members of the prefecture always attend the pope on his travels.

Pontifical Chapel and Pontifical Family. These two groups make up the papal court in the original sense of retainers gathered about a monarch. They are constituted by higher officers of the Curia, by heads of religious orders, by papal servants – active or honorary – by gentlemen ushers, by assistants at the papal throne, by papal chaplains and so on.

Office for Pontifical Ceremonies has been in existence since the 5th century to oversee religious services in which either the pope himself or high officers of the Curia are involved.

Introduction

Pontifical Chapel of Music. Groups of musicians have been associated with the papacy from time immemorial. The Pontifical Chapel is the formal name for the Sistine Choir.

Swiss Guard. Mercenaries, many of them Swiss, were employed in the papal armies from the 15th century onwards, if not earlier, but only the Swiss Guard still survive as a fully constituted corps. The corps has responsibility for the safety of the pope. They depend upon him directly, but by arrangement they are also at the service of the Vatican City for police and security duties. As presently constituted the corps has a full establishment of 100 men, of whom four are officers and two are drummers. The commanding officer has the rank of colonel and is a member of the Pontifical Family.

Welfare Service of the Holy Father has its origins in the traditional care for the poor, orphans and widows of the city of Rome undertaken by the bishop of the city.

Archive of the Second Vatical Council.

Personnel Office of the Holy See, set up in 1971 to improve relations with those who work in the Vatican.

Pontifical academies

Pontifical Academy of St. Thomas Aquinas and of the Catholic Religion. The Academy of the Catholic Religion was founded in 1801 and the Academy of St. Thomas in 1879 (by a pope eager to encourage the study of Thomas's theology).

Pontifical Roman Theological Academy was founded at the end of the 17th century and approved at the beginning of the 18th. It has been open to membership by theologians from all over the world since 1956.

Pontifical Academy of Our Lady Immaculate was founded in 1835, though it achieved its 'pontifical' title only in 1864.

Pontifical and International Marian Academy was founded in 1946, 'pontifical' since 1959.

Distinguished Artistic Academy of Scholars at the Pantheon founded in 1543.

Pontifical Academy of Archaeology has its origins in the 15th century but, after various changes of name, it was given its pontifical title in 1829. It is concerned with the history of ancient and mediaeval art, as well as archaeology.

College of Devotion to the Martyrs was founded in 1879.

Pontifical Academy of Sciences was founded in 1603 but was given its present name only in 1936. Its seat, since 1922, has been the Casino of Pius IV. The seventy academicians are selected from every scientific discipline, and from every country in the world. No form of discrimination whatever is applied, which makes this academy unique of its kind.

Pontifical Ecclesiastical Academy was founded in 1701 and was known until recently as the Pontifical Academy of Noble Ecclesiastics. Its purpose is to train young priests for the papal diplomatic service, and although listed here by the *Annuario* it is really an educational institution.

Institute for the Work of Religion is also out of place here, since it is not an 'academy' but a bank. It is what is known to the world at large as the Vatican Bank. The Administration of the Work of Religion was begun in 1887 to gather funds for the work of the Church around the world. Its present name was given it in 1942, when its role was widened to allow it to hold money on behalf of religious orders, charitable institutions and so on. It acts both as a merchant bank and, for people associated with the Vatican, a clearing bank.

Pilgrimage to the Chair of Peter was founded in 1933 and given full autonomy in 1972. Its purpose is to help poorer pilgrims to Rome in particular, and to the shrines of Italy in general.

Pontifical Institute 'Notre Dame of Jerusalem Centre' was set up in 1884 as a way of helping French people travel to the Holy Land, but its scope was broadened in 1973, and it was given its new name in 1978.

Pius XII Foundation for the Apostolate of the Laity was established in 1933 and reorganized in 1972 to administer money intended to promote the apostolate of the laity. It is supervised by the Secretariat of State.

'Latinitas' Foundation was set up in 1976 to promote the study of the Latin language and literature, especially in the ecclesiastical sphere.

In addition to these academies of one sort of another, the *Annuario* lists 'cultural institutes', by which it means universities and other

Introduction

'institutes of higher learning' both in Rome and around the world. Of these the most important is undoubtedly the Gregorian University with its associated Biblical and Oriental Institutes. Mention of it will be found elsewhere in the bibliography. There is also in the pages of the *Annuario* a lengthy list of 'colleges' which, for the most part, provide residential facilities and some tutorial help to students attending classes at the Gregorian and elsewhere. The Beda, the English, the Scots and the North American colleges are noted in the bibliography as being of especial interest to British and American readers. The German and Ethiopian Colleges may be within the confines of the Vatican City, the Gregorian University on tax-exempt property of the Holy See, but to discuss these further would be to stray too far from the purpose of this introduction.

Laid out above are the main structures of the bureaucracy of the Vatican City State with its 1,400 employees, and of the Roman Curia with some 3,000. The presentation has, for the most part, been schematic. Greater detail about the lives of those who live and work in and around the Vatican City will be found in several of the books listed at the beginning of this bibliography. George Bull's *Inside the Vatican* is the most recent, and so in some ways the most useful, but it must be remembered that all accounts — like all bibliographies — are dated as soon as they are published. The Holy See is the product (under God, a Catholic would want to add) of 2,000 years of history, and it has not stopped changing yet.

The City and Its Citizens

1 **Inside the Vatican.**
George Bull.   London: Hutchinson, 1982. 293p. 2 maps.
bibliog.

Mr. Bull provides a rapid survey of the Vatican - its buildings, its personalities, its eccentricities. Although it is probably the most up-to-date description of the working of the Vatican City State, drawn from conversations with many of those most closely involved in the running of the affairs of the Church, it is by no means a replacement for Poupard's more sober and schematic account in *Connaissance du Vatican* (q.v.), despite the fact that the latter is by now rather out of date. Bull provides a useful series of appendixes listing the offices, and the names of some of the office-holders, of the various departments which go to make up the administration of the Roman Church and the Vatican State.

2 **The pope's divisions.**
Peter Nichols.   London; Boston, Massachusetts: Faber & Faber, 1981. 382p.

The greater part of this book by the Rome correspondent of *The Times* is concerned with the Roman Catholic Church as a whole. However, chapters 4 to 7 inclusive are accounts of the papacy, the Vatican City, and the Roman Curia. Though briefer and necessarily less detailed than, for example, the above account by George Bull, Nichols is considerably less in awe of the system - he is not a Catholic himself, though married to one - and more perceptive.

3 **Le Vatican.** (The Vatican.)
Paul Poupard.   Paris: Presses Universitaires de France, 1981.
125p. maps.

Mgr. Poupard is one of the best guides to the Vatican City and its workings. This little book is a mass of compressed information, and includes excellent plans both of the Basilica of St. Peter's and of the whole Vatican City.

The City and Its Citizens

4 The Vatican papers.
Nino Lo Bello. Dunton Green, England: New English Library, 1982. 246p. bibliog.

A collection of, for the most part, rather unpleasant short pieces about aspects of the Vatican's life and culture. It has, overall, something of the taste of a prolonged gossip column. There are, however, brief informative pieces on the Vatican Radio, the Vatican's newspaper and its observatory which are reasonably straightforward and worth looking at since so little else is available.

5 The anatomy of the Catholic Church.
Gerard Noel. London: Hodder & Stoughton, 1980. 288p. bibliog.

By far the greater part of this book is a fairly summary and rather general survey of modern Catholicism. There is, however, a brief chapter (chapter 10) on the papacy which provides useful background information about the institution for anyone with a limited amount of time at his or her disposal, and there is an excellent section (chapter 16, entitled 'Clerico-capitalism') on the Vatican's financial situation.

6 Daily life in the Vatican.
Peter Nichols. In: *The Vatican*. Photographed by Fred Mayer. New York: Vendome Press; Dublin: Gill & Macmillan, 1980, p. 105-12.

A succinct and attractively written account of what it is like to be a citizen of the Vatican City State, or to work within its confines.

7 The secrets of the Vatican.
Douglas Sladen. London: Hurst & Blackett, 1907. 505p.

The particular value of this book lies in its discursive account of life in the papal court at the end of the 19th and the beginning of the 20th centuries, including descriptions of papal ceremonial. The volume takes in everything, from what happens when a pope dies, through a detailed narrative of a pope's daily routine and the workings of the Roman Curia, to descriptions of the library and museums.

8 Vatican assignment.
Alec Randall. London: Heinemann, 1956. 210p.

The author, who closed his diplomatic career as British ambassador in Denmark, served in the British legation to the Holy See during the period which saw the rise of Mussolini and the signing of the Lateran Treaty. His book portrays the work of the legation, describes some of the personalities involved in the running of Vatican affairs, and outlines the system of government then prevailing, before becoming something of a travelogue.

9 The Vatican yesterday - today - tomorrow.
George Seldes. London: Kegan Paul, 1934. 439p.

The tone of this book is very much that of the mid-1930s when, by all outward signs, the Vatican was at its most self-confident. Though the author shares this self-confidence, his book contains a good deal of incidental information about the running of the Vatican (on the finances, for example) which is useful. There is a good chapter on the work of the Roman Rota in dissolving marriages at the time, and an entertaining one on papal courtiers.

10 The genius of the Vatican.
Robert Sencourt. London: Jonathan Cape, 1935. 315p. bibliog.

Sencourt's book covers the Vatican's history and politics, but has little to say about its religious significance or its internal organization. However, because the author manages to represent the Holy See very much, one imagines, in the way in which it saw itself in the mid-1930s, the book is interesting as an historical document.

11 Report from the Vatican.
Bernard Wall. London: Weidenfeld & Nicolson, 1956. 247p.

Mr. Wall has written a discursive study of the Vatican in its entirety, from its art to its politics. Obviously the book is now, several popes and a council later, rather dated, but Mr. Wall was a highly perceptive observer.

12 The Vatican from within.
Corrado Pallenberg. New York: Hawthorn Books; London: Harrap, 1961. 271p. bibliog.

Pallenberg outlines his own religious position in the introduction: he was baptized a Lutheran, but now owes allegiance to no particular denomination. This, he claims, gives him 'relative impartiality'. There is, nonetheless, an edge to his account of the Vatican - see, for example, the chapter entitled 'How a marriage is annulled'. No secrets are revealed, but full of useful information.

13 The world of the Vatican.
Robert Neville. New York: Harper & Row, 1962. 256p.

A mixture: the lives of Pius XII and of John XXIII intermingled with studies of the Vatican itself, well put together by a journalist who for some years headed the Time-Life bureau in Rome. He is interesting on the Vatican's organization ('The shell of sovereignty') and, not surprisingly, particularly good on the Vatican's attitude to the media ('News-gathering at the Vatican').

14 The Vatican and Christian Rome.
Rome: Libreria Editrice Vaticana, 1975. 522p. bibliog.

Two-thirds of this massive, and splendidly illustrated, volume is concerned with the Vatican City itself. Much of the remainder is devoted to Rome's churches and catacombs. The series of essays which make up the text deal, in some instances, with parts of the Vatican City upon which little else is available, and these are noted elsewhere in this bibliography. Among the many pictures are photographs of works of art and of manuscripts as well as the more customary views: an excellent collection for browsing through.

15 **The Vatican.**
   Photographed by Fred Mayer.   New York: Vendome Press;
   Dublin: Gill & Macmillan, 1980. 223p. map.

Fred Mayer is a photographer rather than an author, and has here pictured the
Vatican at work. His book contains the usual selection of photographs of great
events and of noble works of art, but it is even more concerned with displaying
the everyday working bureaucracy of the Holy See. It is an unexpected view of a
much photographed world. A useful map of the Vatican is included.

Guides for Visitors

The Vatican City

16 The Vatican City.
Eugenio Pucci. Florence, Italy: Bonechi-Edizioni 'Il
Turismo', 1979. 159p. map.

Much of the Vatican City is closed to visitors, some of it is open only to those in
possession of special passes. Pucci's thorough guide makes some reference to that
which is invisible, and briefly describes what may be seen on special occasions.
For the most part, however, he limits himself to historical and artistic notes about
what may be seen by the ordinary visitor. Not surprisingly, the longest section is
devoted to the Sistine Chapel. The whole guide is generously illustrated with
colour reproductions, and there is a map (folded loose in a plastic cover) of the
Vatican City plus a detailed plan of St. Peter's. The English is somewhat idiosyncratic, and the book is full of typographical errors. The guide is arranged in the
form of a series of itineraries, and conveniently sized to slip into a jacket pocket.

17 How to see the Vatican.
Douglas Sladen. London: Kegan Paul; New York: James
Pitt, 1914. 441p.

Not all of the Vatican City is open to tourists. Sladen's book serves as a guide to
the Vatican Palace, to its decoration and its art, and has much to say about those
sections of the palace usually closed to visitors.

18 Exploring the Vatican.
James A. Van der Veldt. London: Hollis & Carter, 1947.
188p.

This is something of a curiosity. It is an informal account of the Vatican City, its
art, its history and its organization, presented through the eyes of the young son
of the American ambassador to the Holy See, forced to spend four years of the
Second World War within the Vatican walls.

5

Rome and the Vatican

19 **Rome and its environs.**
Edited by Alta Macadam. London: Ernest Benn; Chicago: Rand McNally, 1979. 2nd ed. 402p. map. (Blue Guide).

There is an excellent brief description of the Vatican City State opening the section on St. Peter's and the Vatican in this guidebook. It is informative on the art treasures to be found in the various museums, and even on parts of the city state not normally open to visitors.

20 **Rome.**
Lausanne, Switzerland: Berlitz, 1982. rev. ed. 128p.

The Berlitz guide to Rome is distributed in the United Kingdom and the United States by Macmillan, and is therefore readily available in its English version. It is very brief, but is a convenient size for the pocket and has good, practical information about the Vatican as well, of course, as on Rome in general. It is no substitute for a proper guidebook, but can be used for on-the-spot information when a fuller book has been left behind.

21 **The Christian's guide to Rome.**
S. G. A. Luff. London: Burns & Oates, 1967. 299p. maps.

A fairly substantial, traditional guide to Christian Rome, based upon the author's four years' experience of showing tourists the Christian sights. There is perhaps not as much as one might have expected about the Vatican itself.

22 **The pilgrim's guide to Rome.**
Henry Vidon. London: Sheed & Ward, 1975. 217p.

This somewhat informally written guidebook is designed specifically with English and American visitors in mind. It briefly surveys the historical connections between England and Rome and then, in a series of tours ('On your way to St. Peter's', 'From Trastevere to the Piazza della Minerva' and so on), it details churches, monuments and events which have a particular significance for the Anglo-Saxon world.

23 **A companion guide to Rome.**
Georgina Masson. London: Collins, 1980. 6th ed. 541p. map. bibliog.

Less than 100 pages are devoted to the Vatican City, and those, like the rest of the book, are organized by very sensible itineraries. Good accounts of what is to be seen, with adequate historical information. A wholly unscientific survey by a Rome resident suggested that this was the most popular guidebook to the city.

24 **Rome.**
Anthony Pereira. London: Batsford, 1974. 351p. map. bibliog.

There is a strong stress on the ecclesiastical aspects of the city in Pereira's account, with a good deal of historical background. There are two chapters on St.

Peter's and the Vatican, and a brief section on the work of Bernini, though not giving especial emphasis to his work on the Vatican.

25 Our islands and Rome.
Edmund O'Gorman. Alcester, England; Dublin: C. Goodliffe Neale, 1974. 178p.

The islands in question are, of course, the British Isles, and Fr. O'Gorman picks out places in Rome of especial interest to British and Irish tourists. His style is gossippy, but there is a good deal of historical information to be had from the book with relatively little effort.

26 A traveller in Rome.
H. V. Morton. London: Methuen, 1957. 432p. bibliog.

Morton is, of course, a skilled travel writer and a pleasure to read. He devotes chapter 10 (p. 355-89) to the Vatican City, and his brief account is as evocative as many a longer one. Oddments of information about the Vatican and its inhabitants are also to be found scattered elsewhere throughout the book.

27 Rome and the Vatican.
E. Mansione, L. Pazienti. London: Frederick Muller, 1982. 128p.

Obviously only a part of this attractively produced book is directly concerned with the Vatican (p. 78-124), but it also contains accounts of three of Rome's churches most caught up in papal history: Santa Maria Maggiore, St. Paul's Outside the Walls, and Rome's cathedral church of St. John Lateran. A few pages are also devoted to Castel San'Angelo, now of course outside the Vatican City State but once central to papal defences. The format of the book makes it impracticable as a guidebook, but read before a visit it would make an excellent introduction to Christian Rome.

Archaeology

28 The Roman catacombs and their martyrs.
Ludwig Hertling, Engelbert Kirschbaum.   London: Darton,
Longman & Todd; Milwaukee, Wisconsin: Bruce, 1960. rev.
ed. 274p. map.

The interest of this book is rather wider than the title suggests: it is an excellent
introduction and guidebook to the archaeology of Rome and the Vatican City. It
interprets the findings of the archaeologists, and indicates their significance for
the history of Christian Rome.

29 The catacombs: rediscovered monuments of early Christianity.
J. Stevenson.   London: Thames & Hudson, 1978. 179p. map.
bibliog.

As a background to early Christian Rome, some knowledge of the catacombs, the
burial-places of Christians for three centuries and more, is essential. This book is
rather narrower in scope than that of Hertling and Kirschbaum above, but does
not confine itself strictly to Rome and its environs.

30 The tombs of St. Peter and St. Paul.
Engelbert Kirschbaum.   London: Secker & Warburg, 1959.
247p.

Fr. Kirschbaum was one of the archaeologists responsible for the excavations
beneath the Basilica of St. Peter's. This account of the pagan necropolis found
under the church, and of the tomb of St. Peter, therefore has an especial authority. Only chapter 5, p. 165-94, is exclusively devoted to excavations at St. Paul's
Outside the Walls.

31 The shrine of St. Peter and the Vatican excavations.
Jocelyn Toynbee, John Ward Perkins.   London, New York:
Longman, Green, 1956. 292p. bibliog.

Two English experts provide, for an English-speaking (and non-professional)
readership, a detailed account of the Vatican excavations. The excellent text is
liberally illustrated with photographs and plans.

32 **The tomb of St. Peter.**
Margherita Guarducci. London: Harrap; New York:
Hawthorn, 1960. 198p. bibliog.
Particularly concerned with the epigraphical evidence - controversial.

33 **Le reliquie di Pietro sotto la confessione della basilica
Vaticana.** (The relics of Peter beneath the confession in the
Vatican basilica.)
Margherita Guarducci. Rome: Libreria Editrice Vaticana,
1965. 182p.
The 'confession' is the horseshoe-shaped cavity before the high altar in St. Peter's,
leading to the supposed tomb of the apostle Peter. Although this book has Professor Guarducci's name on the title-page, over half of it has been contributed by
others - in particular by Venerando Correnti - and consists of a detailed account
of the finds under St. Peter's, especially of the human remains.

34 **The bones of St. Peter.**
John Evangelist Walsh. New York: Doubleday, 1982. 218p.
This book was not yet available when the bibliography was completed, so its
distinctiveness is not easy to assess. It is billed by its publishers as a 'fascinating
account, never before released in the U.S., of the excavations beneath St. Peter's
and the quest for the bones of Simon bar-Jonah', i.e., St. Peter. It would seem,
however, that the book will offer a readily accessible version of the complex story
of the archaeological finds beneath the basilica.

35 **Pagan and Christian Rome.**
Rodolfo Lanciani. London: Macmillan, 1895. 374p.
Obviously this book is now much out of date, but Lanciani's study of how a
pagan city became a Christian one retains considerable interest, not least because
of the author's method. His simply deals in one chapter with, for example, pagan
tombs, and in the next with papal ones.

History

The city of Rome

36 **Naissance d'une hiérarchie.** (Birth of a hierarchy.)
Alexandre Faivre. Paris: Beauchesne, 1977. 443p. bibliog.
(Théologie Historique 40).
The greater part of this book is a legal and historical study of the origins of the hierarchy as it came to be established in the early centuries of the Christian Church. Faivre treats specifically of the structures of the Church in Rome on p. 299-370. Some of the clerical grades which emerged came to play a role in the civil, as well as in the religious, life of the city.

37 **Rome in the Dark Ages.**
Peter Llewellyn. London: Faber, 1970. 324p. bibliog.
Part story of the papacy, part history of the city, Llewellyn's book is a splendid evocation of the period 500-1,000.

38 **History of the city of Rome in the Middle Ages.**
Ferdinand Gregorovius. London: G. Bell, 1900-09. 2nd ed.,
rev. 8 vols.
Although much in need of correction in matters of detail, this major work is still worth consulting for the period it covers - from the 5th to the 16th centuries. It is concerned with the political history of the city, rather than the history of the papacy, though the two inevitably are intertwined.

39 **History of Rome and the popes in the Middle Ages.**
Hartmann Grisar. London: Kegan Paul, 1911-12. 3 vols.
The author had intended to produce a six-volume study, but he only wrote the first of them - and this was published in three volumes in the English edition. Fr. Grisar wrote quite explicitly that his work was an apologetic riposte to Gregorovius (see above) who had, Grisar believed, given far too little attention to the papacy. In Grisar's version the popes occupy centre-stage. He covers only the

period to the 8th century, but is a useful source of information on the art and archaeology of Rome during that period.

40 Pilgrimage: an image of mediaeval religion.
Jonathan Sumption.   London: Faber, 1975. 391p. bibliog.

Chapter 13 of *Pilgrimage* recounts why people went to Rome in the Middle Ages, and what happened to them when they got there. It is important to understand Rome and the papacy as being the centres of pilgrimage.

41 Rome before Avignon.
Robert Brentano.   New York: Basic Books; London:
Longman, 1974. 340p.

Brentano subtitles his book 'a social history of thirteenth-century Rome'. He discusses the layout of the city (his book overlaps with the final pages of Kraut-heimer's *Rome: profile of a city,* q.v.), its organization and government, the role of the papacy within it, and the life of the common people.

42 Renaissance Rome.
Peter Partner.   Berkeley, California; London: University of
California Press, 1976. 241p. bibliog.

By 'Renaissance Rome' is meant the years 1500-59. There is considerable cove-rage of the life of the people of the city, but the main emphasis is upon the popes, papal policy and cultural achievement, and life at the papal court.

43 The sack of Rome, 1527.
Judith Hook.   London: Macmillan, 1972. 343p. 2 maps.
bibliog.

The capture of Rome by the Emperor Charles V had a profound effect upon the history of Europe, not least upon the marriage plans of Henry VIII and therefore upon the course of England's religious development. Dr. Hook's detailed study reveals the tensions within Rome's great families and the problems facing the administrators of the Papal States, as well as presenting the emperor's campaign against the papacy within the framework of the history of Europe.

44 The sack of Rome, 1527.
André Chastel.   Princeton, New Jersey: Princeton University
Press, 1982. c.430p. (Bollingen Series 35: 26).

At the time of completing this bibliography, Chastel's book had not yet appeared. The author's reputation, however, and the renown of the series of lectures for which the text was originally prepared (the A. W. Mellon Lectures in the Fine Arts for 1977), are sufficient guarantee of the quality of the work. According to the advance notices, Professor Chastel concentrates on the cultural consequences of the sack. Of particular interest will be his reflections upon the way in which popes used artists to reassert the legitimacy of their temporal power.

45 **Vie économique et sociale de Rome dans la seconde moitié du XVIe siècle.** (Economic and social life at Rome during the second half of the 16th century.)
Jean Delumeau. Paris: Brocard, 1957-59. 2 vols. bibliog.
(Bibliothèque des Ecoles Françaises d'Athènes et de Rome, 184).

An outstanding study of every aspect of Roman life, picking up the story of the city more or less at the point at which Peter Partner's much slimmer volume *Renaissance Rome* (q.v.) breaks off. Part 1 takes in the building of the city, and part 2 deals with, among other things, the papacy's financial problems.

46 **Rome au XVIe siècle.** (Rome in the 16th century.)
Jean Delumeau. Paris: Hachette, 1975. 247p. bibliog.

A summary of Delumeau's major work on Rome, listed above - considerably more readable.

47 **Daily life in papal Rome in the eighteenth century.**
Maurice Andrieux. London: Allen & Unwin, 1968. 223p. bibliog.

An attractive, entertaining book about social and religious life in Rome in the period just before the French Revolution changed it for ever. A good deal on the interconnection between papal court and Roman society.

48 **La vita religiosa a Roma intorno al 1870.** (Religious life at Rome around the year 1870.)
Edited by P. Droulers, G. Martina, P. Tufari. Rome: Università Gregoriana Editrice, 1971. 273p. (Miscellanea Historiae Pontificiae, 31).

Rather wider in scope than the title might suggest, this collection of essays by a number of scholars examines the effect of the fall of Rome in 1870 upon the inhabitants of the city.

49 **Peter's city.**
Thomas Ewing Moore. London: Harding & More, 1929. 284p. map. bibliog.

Though in general this book about life in Rome before and after the concordat, written by an American diplomat, has little to offer that might not be found elsewhere, it has interesting snippets on fascism in Italy, on Castel Gandolfo, and the texts of the Lateran Treaty, the concordat with Italy, the financial convention, the Law of Guarantees of 1871, and other useful documents.

50 **Roma 'città sacra'?** (Rome: a 'holy city'?)
Andrea Riccardi. Milan, Italy: Vita e Pensiero, 1979. 414p. (Cultura e Storia, Nuova Serie, 3).

The author explains in his preface that he has come across, in addresses given by ecclesiastics during the 1930s and 1940s, the ideology of Rome as a holy city.

Riccardi sticks closely to his theme, but provides an insight into the Vatican and Italian politics both before and after the Second World War.

51 **Roman century, 1870-1970.**
J. R. Glorney Bolton. London: Hamish Hamilton, 1970. 306p. bibliog.
A discursively written, non-technical account - but none the worse for that - of the relationship between the Vatican and the city of Rome from the time that city ceased to be exclusively a papal concern. A useful introduction.

Roman Catholicism

52 **Histoire de l'Eglise.** (History of the Church.)
Founded by Augustin Fliche, Victor Martin. Paris: Bloud et Gray, 1934-64. 21 vols.
This series' 'founder editors' have rather given their name to the whole production: it is known familiarly as 'Fliche-Martin'. It is probably the most comprehensive of the readily obtainable histories of the Church, though alas only a very small proportion of it has been translated into English. The earliest sections to be written are obviously now somewhat dated, though even they have much to recommend them, and the final volume takes the story no further than the death of Pius IX in 1878.

53 **History of the Church.**
Edited by Hubert Jedin. London: Burns & Oates, 1980-81. 10 vols. bibliog.
The papacy is, of course, the highest office in the Roman Catholic Church, and though it may be studied separately from Catholicism, it cannot be properly understood except in the context of general Church history. This set of volumes is the most comprehensive to have appeared in English in recent years (some volumes were originally published in the 1960s under the title of *Handbook of Church history*). There are detailed lists of contents to each volume, which makes for ease in consultation, and though it is somewhat short on analysis, most necessary information may be rapidly found. On the other hand it has a number of drawbacks of which users should be aware: it has been accused of being too Catholic in its bias; the bibliographies, which are extensive and a major selling-point, cater for the original German, rather than new English, readers; and the authors have given a distinct emphasis to matters German, rather to the detriment of other countries. However, despite the delay in publishing the translations of some of the volumes, coverage in the final volume comes right down to modern times.

54 **The Christian centuries.**
London: Darton, Longman & Todd, 1964- . 5 vols. bibliog.
The Christian centuries is something of an Anglo-French production, and the delay in its appearance may perhaps be caused by the difficulties inherent in organizing the large number of scholarly contributions. But the volumes so far published (1, 2 and 5) have been well worth waiting for, especially the fifth

volume which brings the history down to Vatican II. It is much stronger on analysis than the preceding comparable German production, and the bibliographies, though not as extensive as in that collection, are at least more slanted towards an English-speaking readership.

55 A concise history of the Church.
August Franzen, revised and edited by John P. Dolan. New York: Herder & Herder; London: Burns & Oates, 1969. 462p.

Possibly the best one-volume, and readily intelligible, history of the Catholic Church in English. No great panoply of scholarship, no bibliography, and a shortish index, but a detailed list of contents which makes for relatively easy reference.

56 A short history of the Catholic Church.
Philip Hughes. London: Burns & Oates, 1974. 8th ed. 310p.

Mgr. Hughes' original text has, in this edition, a 'final chapter' written by E. E. Y. Hales covering the years 1939-65, and a 'postscript' for the years 1966-74. Not recommended quite as much as the above item by Franzen for a short introduction or quick reference book, but perhaps likely to be more readily available since Hughes was a well-known scholar, especially in the area of Reformation studies.

The Papal State

57 The beginnings of the temporal sovereignty of the popes.
Louis Duchesne. London: Kegan Paul, 1908. 312p.

The classic study of the first centuries (754-1073) of the Papal State. It was written by a Catholic priest whose loyalty to the truth as he found it in history brought him into conflict with his ecclesiastical superiors.

58 Consul of God: the life and times of Gregory the Great.
Jeffrey Richards. London; Boston, Massachusetts: Routledge & Kegan Paul, 1980. 309p. bibliog.

Recommended not so much as a biography of one of the papacy's most interesting incumbents, but as an easily accessible account of the origins of the Papal States. This is a topic that recurs throughout the book, but especially on p. 85-139.

59 The lands of St. Peter.
Peter Partner. London: Eyre Methuen, 1972. 471p. bibliog.

Most histories of the papacy concentrate either upon the growth of the papal office as such, or on the development of papal government. Dr. Partner's very readable, but scholarly, book studies the expansion of the Papal States, the forerunners of the Vatican City, from their origins about the time of Pope Gregory the Great (the end of the 6th century) to approximately the middle of the 15th century. He therefore chronicles the involvement of the papacy in political, rather than in religious, history.

60 **The Malatesta of Rimini and the Papal State.**
P. J. Jones.   Cambridge, England: Cambridge University Press, 1974. 372p. map. bibliog.

A detailed political history of part - but a major part - of the Papal States from the 13th to the early 16th centuries, and of the clashes between successive popes and their supposed subjects the Malatesta, one of mediaeval Italy's most colourful families.

61 **The Papal State in the thirteenth century.**
Daniel Waley.   London: Macmillan; New York: St. Martin's Press, 1961. 355p. map. bibliog.

Waley regards the election of Pope Innocent III in 1198 as heralding the real beginning of the Papal State. His study is informative about the organization of the state as well as its place in European politics. His first chapter contains an outline history down to the election of Innocent.

62 **The Papal State under Martin V.**
Peter Partner.   London: British School at Rome, 1958. 264p. map. bibliog.

In Dr. Partner's judgement, Martin V 'rescued the Papal State from the chaos into which it had fallen'. If, as Waley believes in the above entry, Innocent III was the first founder of the state, Martin, pope from 1417-31, could be claimed as its second. The first forty pages provide an outline history up to Martin's election.

63 **Italy in the making.**
G. F.-H. Berkeley, J. Berkeley.   Cambridge, England: Cambridge University Press, 1933-40. 3 vols. maps. bibliog.

Covering the period 1815-48 this detailed history of the unification of Italy up to the Year of Revolutions has a considerable amount, especially in volumes 2 and 3, on the final years of the Papal States.

The 'Roman Question'

64 **The Roman Question and the powers, 1848-65.**
Ivan Scott.   The Hague: Nijhoff, 1969. 390p. bibliog.

A detailed study of the effect upon the other major European states of the unification of Italy and the fall of the Papal States.

65 The Roman Question: extracts from the despatches of Odo Russell from Rome, 1858-70.
Noel Blakiston.   London: Chapman & Hall, 1962. 474p.

Odo Russell, who died in Berlin while serving as ambassador there, was at the British embassy in Rome from 1858-70. His vivid accounts, contained in the despatches sent to the Foreign Office in London, of the political and ecclesiastical intrigue surrounding the pope at the very end of the Papal States make fascinating reading.

66 Le due Rome. (The two Romes.)
Giovanni Spadolini.   Florence, Italy: Felice le Monnier, 1975. 3rd ed. 631p. bibliog.

A massive study, liberally illustrated with caricatures and cartoons and adorned with an impressive bibliography, of the 'Roman Question' from the time of Napoleon to the Lateran Treaty - though it strays beyond - by an expert in the intricacies of Italian politics.

67 Church and state in fascist Italy.
D. A. Binchy.   London, New York: Oxford University Press, 1941. 774p. bibliog.

A highly respected, very detailed study of the settlement of the 'Roman Question', and the consequences of the settlement up to the outbreak of the Second World War.

The papacy

68 Keepers of the keys.
Nicolas Cheetham.   London: Macdonald, 1982. 340p. bibliog.

Sir Nicolas has written a fairly uncomplicated, straight narrative history of the Roman pontiffs. He rather avoids the difficult bits, like the early history of the bishopric of Rome, but brings the story down to the assassination attempt on Pope John Paul II. It is not a demanding book, and could profitably be read as a first introduction to the history of the papacy or as a means of establishing a general background knowledge before visiting Rome.

69 The decline and fall of the Roman Church.
Malachi Martin.   Toronto: Academic Press, 1981; London: Secker & Warburg, 1982. 309p.

An interesting, novelesque, and alternative view of the history of the papacy. Not wholly to be trusted in detail, but nonetheless a view of the 'decline and fall' of the papacy which is shared by many adherents of Roman Catholicism and, one suspects, by many who are close to the pope himself.

70 **A history of the popes.**
Fernand Hayward.   London: J. M. Dent, 1931. 405p.
A competent, straightforward history of the papacy. It was very popular in its time, but it is now inevitably somewhat dated. A particularly useful feature, however, is the 'Chronological list of the Roman pontiffs' which is unusual in containing details of their burial-places and, where applicable, monuments.

71 **The popes: a concise biographical history.**
Eric John.   London: Burns & Oates, 1964. 496p. bibliog.
Essay-length surveys of different periods of papal history interspersed among the lives of the popes, arranged in chronological order. The end-papers illustrate the papal coats of arms from Boniface VIII to Paul VI (i.e. from 1294 to 1978). A useful quick reference book.

72 **An illustrated history of the popes.**
Michael Walsh.   London: Marshall Cavendish; New York:
St. Martin's Press, 1980. 256p. bibliog.
This is a popular account of the growth of the papal office. It is told through the lives of many - though not of all - of the holders of the papal title, and aims to show the non-specialist reader how it was that the papacy came to play so dominant a role in the history of Christianity. At the end of the book there is a list of popes and antipopes recording their nationality and year of birth, where known, as well as the date of their election and of their death or deposition.

73 **The papacy: an illustrated history from St. Peter to Paul VI.**
Christopher Hollis.   London: Weidenfeld & Nicolson, 1964.
304p.
Although the compilers of this book constitute a distinguished group of scholars, the brevity of each contribution is a drawback. It is still a a valuable quick reference book, and in addition to the history of the popes there are sections on St. Peter's and on the Vatican Palace.

74 **The popes and the papacy in the early Middle Ages 476-752.**
Jeffrey Richards.   London; Boston, Massachusetts: Routledge
& Kegan Paul, 1979. 422p. bibliog.
A somewhat polemical, but in general very useful, history of the early mediaeval papacy.

75 **A short history of the papacy in the Middle Ages.**
Walter Ullmann.   London: Methuen, 1972. 389p.
An excellent little book, provided that the reader remembers that Ullmann's especial interests, which tend to dominate, are in legal and administrative developments. The period covered is from the 5th to the 15th centuries, with brief excursuses before and after.

76 Medieval papalism.
Walter Ullmann. London: Methuen, 1949. 230p. bibliog.

The papacy in the context of mediaeval political theory - or, at least, mediaeval political theory as it was conceived of by Church lawyers. An important book for papal ideology.

77 The lives of the popes.
Horace K. Mann. London: Routledge & Kegan Paul, 1902-32; Wilmington, North Carolina: Consortium Books, 197[8?]. 18 vols. bibliog.

Fr. Mann began his work to complement Pastor's *History of the popes* (q.v.), and so his period extends from the reign of Gregory the Great, elected in 590, to the death of Benedict XI in 1304. Although he was dealing with much more difficult sources than Pastor, Mann always manages to tell his story in an interesting fashion, and he is well worth reading. His work, however, has never attained the status of Pastor's, and has in part been replaced by individual biographies and other studies.

78 Western society and the Church in the Middle Ages.
R. W. Southern. Harmondsworth, England: Penguin Books, 1970. 376p. (Pelican History of the Church, no. 2).

The fourth chapter of Professor Southern's outstanding little book is devoted to the papacy, from 'The primitive age, c.700-c.1050', through 'The age of growth, c.1050-c.1300' to 'The inflationary spiral, c.1300-c.1520', in all some eighty pages. Southern's account of the history of the mediaeval papacy not only has the advantage of being brief, but is also a neat contrast with the more legalistic approach adopted by Ullmann (q.v.).

79 The medieval papacy.
Geoffrey Barraclough. London: Thames & Hudson, 1968. 216p. bibliog.

For Barraclough, apparently, the mediaeval papacy begins in the middle of the 8th century and ends at the start of the 16th, though in the first twenty or so pages he provides an outline history from the very earliest times. This is an excellent short account, and the number of illustrations reduce the length of the text considerably, to make it a very manageable book. Many other studies of the mediaeval popes lay stress on the legal framework of their authority, this one stresses the influence of social and political factors.

80 The popes at Avignon, 1305-78.
G. Mollat. London: Thomas Nelson, 1963. 361p. bibliog.

The classic study of what became known as 'the Babylonian captivity' - though what was odd about the years in Avignon was not that the pope was living outside Rome but that he stayed so long in one place.

81 **The history of the popes.**
Ludwig von Pastor. London: Routledge & Kegan Paul,
1891-1953. 40 vols.

The story of Pastor's labours in writing his *History* is itself worthy of study, and is briefly told in Owen Chadwick's *Catholicism and history* (q.v.). His mammoth work seems sometimes an almost day-by-day, if not hour-by-hour, account of the popes and of the papal court from 1304 to 1799. Immensely learned, and footnoted with ample reference to documentary material, Pastor will remain the standard work for generations to come. Not, however, an easy read.

82 **A Renaissance likeness: art and culture in Raphael's 'Julius II'.**
Loren Partridge, Randolph Starn. Berkeley, California;
London: University of California Press, 1980. 159p. bibliog.

This study of the portrait of Pope Julius II by Raphael, one of the painter's most important works, is imaginatively used by the authors as the starting point for an examination of the Renaissance, Renaissance portraiture in general and papal portraiture in particular, and the role of the papacy during the Renaissance. The emphasis, naturally, is upon the city of Rome.

83 **The history of the popes during the last four centuries.**
Leopold von Ranke. London: George Bell, 1908. 3 vols.

The period covered is from the end of the 15th to the end of the 19th century, and it is dealt with in the first two volumes. The final volume lists the documents von Ranke used, together with extracts from, and comments upon, them. The author was a Lutheran, but this work was epoch-making in the way in which it rose above polemic. It was attacked as too favourable to the Roman Catholics by Protestant historians, and Rome put it on the Index. It was, and remains, a classic work of historiography, though nowadays it is perhaps better known because of Macaulay's review in which he prophesied that one day a New Zealander would be standing on the ruins of Westminster Abbey while the papacy still flourished - a passage beloved by Roman Catholic apologists.

84 **Structure social et l'Eglise.** (Social structure and the Church.)
Marie Zimmermann. Strasbourg, France: Cerdic, 1981.
183p. bibliog.

In practice, of course, the problems of Church-state relationships have to be worked out by local hierarchies, but the prevailing ideology at the Vatican considerably affects the local Church. The author surveys the problem of Church-state relationships from the 18th century to the present day.

85 **The papacy and the modern world.**
Karl Otmar von Aretin. London: Weidenfeld & Nicolson,
1970. 256p. bibliog. (World University Library).

For the author, the 'modern' world begins with the French Revolution. Professor Aretin provides a brief but perceptive account of the problems faced by the papacy in its attempt to come to terms with the 19th and 20th centuries - and with its legacy from the 18th. Emphasis is on political rather than ideological problems.

86 **The Catholic Church in the modern world.**
E. E. Y. Hales. London: Eyre & Spottiswoode, 1958. 332p. bibliog.

While some of this book is concerned with Catholicism in general, a good deal of it presents an excellent survey of the problems of the papacy within the political sphere from Napoleon down to the last years of Pius XII, and of the final years of the Papal States. A good introductory study.

87 **The papacy in the modern world.**
J. Derek Holmes. London: Burns & Oates; New York: Crossroad Publishing, 1981. 275p. bibliog.

For Dr. Holmes the 'modern world' begins with the outbreak of war in 1914. Though some of this book is taken up with religious matters internal to the Catholic Church, most of it is concerned with the relationships between the Vatican and other states on the diplomatic level, and as such it constitutes a useful survey.

88 **The triumph of the Holy See.**
J. Derek Holmes. London: Burns & Oates; Shepherdstown, West Virginia: Patmos, 1978. 306p. bibliog.

A concise history of the papacy during the 19th and early 20th centuries. The author concentrates on papal relations with other European governments, and with Church-state issues in general.

89 **Church and state in Italy 1850-1950.**
A. C. Jemolo. Oxford, England: Blackwell, 1960. 344p.

An abridgement of a much longer work. This version concentrates on those events which have had an influence upon more recent history. Not of course limited to the Vatican, but useful background on the role it plays in Italian politics.

90 **Three popes and a cardinal.**
Malachi Martin. London: Hart-Davies, 1973. 300p.

The three popes of the title are Pius XII, John XXIII and Paul VI. The cardinal is the Jesuit Augustine Bea who served all three and who died, according to the author, 'the most disappointed, embittered, disillusioned and misrepresented member of the Roman Catholic leadership in the twentieth century'. During the intrigues and conspiracies he describes, the author was a Jesuit and teaching, for much of the time, in Rome itself. He presents an idiosyncratic view of the future of the papacy which deserves to be looked at but not necessarily believed.

91 **The utopia of Pope John XXIII.**
Giancarlo Zizola. New York: Orbis, 1978. 379p.

One could recommend this book as a highly intelligent biography of an outstanding ruler of the Vatican City State. For the purposes of this bibliography, however, chapters 1 and 7 and the whole of part 2 constitute a fascinating, if occasionally somewhat speculative, account of the shift in political attitudes in the Vatican in the late 1950s.

92 The papacy in transition.
Patrick Granfield. New York: Doubleday, 1980; Dublin: Gill & Macmillan, 1981. 228p. bibliog.

Granfield's study is basically a theological one. It contains, however, a survey of what might be called the history of papal self-understanding, together with some informed ideas as to ways in which the papacy could evolve in the future. Though it may sometimes appear to have a life of its own, the Vatican bureaucracy exists as a means of carrying out papal policies, and some understanding of the pope's own self-image is essential if one is to appreciate the activities of the state as such.

93 The papacy today.
Francis X. Murphy. London: Weidenfeld & Nicolson, 1981. 269p. bibliog.

The first third or so of this book may safely be disregarded, but it is particularly informative from the election of Pope John XXIII onwards, for the author was a close and perceptive observer of the Vatican scene over that period. He is especially interesting about tensions within the Roman Curia, and their effect on the making of papal policy.

94 The year of the three popes.
Peter Hebblethwaite. London: Collins, 1978. 223p. bibliog.

Although a work of instant history, this is very good of its kind. Hebblethwaite understands the Vatican well, and writes an excellent account of the conclaves of the later summer and early autumn of 1978. He catches the spirit of the events, and describes the issues which were at stake in choosing the Vatican's ruler.

95 The making of the popes.
Andrew M. Greeley. London: Futura, 1979. 302p.

In this curious book Greeley not only records the events surrounding the two conclaves of 1978, but provides a running commentary about his own reactions, emotional and critical, to them. He allows himself much more freedom than does Hebblethwaite in *The year of the three popes* (see above) to speculate about the motives of the cardinals, and about alliances within the conclaves. He also supplies rather more background information.

96 The pope from Poland.
Edited by John Whale. London: Collins, 1980. 270p.

The editor is the religious correspondent of the London *Sunday Times*, and the other four contributors also work, or worked, for that paper. This account of the first fourteen months of the pontificate of John Paul II is therefore put together with considerable journalistic flair, though with uneven success.

97 Pope John Paul II and the Catholic restoration.
Paul Johnson. London: Weidenfeld & Nicolson, 1982. 216p.

It may be that this view of the papacy in modern times is a mistaken one, but it is no less interesting for that. Johnson sees the pontificate of John Paul II so far as an attempt to restore 'order and morale' within the Roman Catholic Church. The present pope has held office for too short a time for it to be entirely clear what his policies will be, and some of the signs are on the face of it contradictory, but Johnson clearly has an empathy with at least one side of the pope's character, which makes this book especially useful despite one's hesitations.

98 **The papal year.**
Peter Hebblethwaite. New York: Macmillan; London: Geoffrey Chapman, 1981. 127p.

An interesting idea: an illustrated account, with perceptive commentary, of a year in the life of the pope - the year in question being, in this case, 1980. The author appears to suggest, on the last page, that it is the first in a series ('there will be another *Papal year*'), but no other has so far materialized.

Language

99 Lexicon eorum vocabulorum quae difficilius Latine redduntur.
(Dictionary of words which are more difficult to turn into Latin.)
Antonio Bacci. Rome: Societas Libreria 'Studium', 1955. 3rd ed. 709p.

Any Latin-English/English-Latin dictionary should in theory be suitable for translating into or out of the language used officially by the Vatican City. The late Cardinal Bacci's *Lexicon*, however, provides guidance when translating modern terms into ecclesiastical Latin. The words, which would not be found in a dictionary of classical Latin of course, are given in Italian in this *Lexicon*. Thus the Italian *bomba atomica* becomes rather pedantically *globus atomica vi* [= force] *displodens*. According to Lo Bello (*The Vatican papers*, q.v., p. 141-45) a new edition is under way, prepared by the Reverend Reginald Foster.

100 Latinitas. (Latinity.)
Vatican City: Libreria Editrice Vaticana. quarterly.

Part of the late Cardinal Bacci's dream to keep Latin alive, this extraordinary journal, the purpose of which is to foster and to improve the use of Latin, even has its advertisements in that language. Its circulation may be small (said to be around 1,000), but that shows a distinct success for such a curiosity.

101 Latin: a historical and linguistic handbook.
Mason Hammond. Cambridge, Massachusetts: Harvard University Press, 1976. 292p. bibliog.

An excellent introduction to the Latin language - including its pronunciation - which takes account of the use of Latin in Church circles. Strictly speaking it is, however, neither a grammar nor, still less, a dictionary, but a very readable study of the language as such.

Language

102 Latin: an intensive course.
Floyd L. Morel, Rita M. Fleischer.   Berkeley, California;
London: University of California Press, 1974. preliminary
ed. 517p.

This constitutes the nearest equivalent to the grammar books which exist in other
languages for the serious-minded business man, and aims to introduce the student
to reading the language as soon as possible. It is, of course, meant for the study
of the classical language, rather than the somewhat debased ecclesiastical form.

103 Latin for local history.
Eileen A. Gooder.   London, New York: Longman, 1978.
2nd ed. 171p.

Mediaeval and Church Latin have much in common. So even if not all of this
book is relevant to the use of the language by the Vatican (e.g. the section on
palaeography) it is still a helpful brief guide.

104 Magna carta latina. (The Latin magna carta.)
Eugen Rosenstock-Huessy, with Fred Lewis
Battles.   Pittsburgh, Pennsylvania: Pickwick Press, 1975.
2nd ed. 296p. bibliog.

Aimed mainly at those interested in singing in Latin, this cheerful introduction to
the language, complete with ample texts for reading purposes, will be of use to
anyone having to use Latin within an ecclesiastical context.

105 Latin can be fun.
Georg Capellanus.   London: Souvenir Press, 1975. 154p.

No doubt intended by its author as something of a joke, this Latin phrase-book,
containing translations for such up-to-date terms as 'indoor aerial' or 'postal
charges', is based at least in part upon Vatican documents. It contains useful, if
rather too abbreviated, lists of geographical terms. No visitor to the Vatican is,
however, expected to speak Latin!

Religion

106 **Enchiridion symbolorum, definitionum et declarationum de rebus fidei et morum.** (A handbook of creeds, definitions, and declaration about faith and morals.) Edited by H. Denzinger, revised and expanded by A. Schönmetzer. Barcelona, Spain; New York: Herder, 1967. 34th ed., rev. 954p.

Those who work within the Vatican City State, and many Roman Catholics the world over, think it is the prime purpose of the Vatican City to provide a central bureaucracy whose purpose is to maintain the Catholic faith in all its purity. There is, however, no clear statement of that faith. This book, known familiarly as 'Denzinger' and constantly referred to in learned footnotes simply as 'DS' (for Denzinger-Schönmetzer), comes nearest to setting out what must, or more often must not, be believed. It contains snippets from councils of the Church, from the writings of eminent theologians, and from the statements of popes arranged in chronological order. There is an outstandingly good index, by means of which an authoritative quotation on every, or almost every, aspect of Catholic faith may be located. Unfortunately no adequate English-language equivalent is available. The text is basically in Latin, though some quotations in other languages, notably Greek, are included.

107 **The Christian faith in the doctrinal documents of the Catholic Church.** Edited by J. Neuner, J. Dupuis. Westminster, Maryland: Christian Classics, 1975. 687p.

This compilation is possibly the nearest thing to Denzinger (see above) which exists in English, though the approach is wholly different. After a preliminary section on professions of the (Catholic) faith, the remaining documents are listed chronologically under themes.

108 Official Catholic teachings.
Wilmington, North Carolina: Consortium Books, 1978. 6
vols.

It is often difficult to find English translations of the more important statements
of popes (apart, now, from encyclicals, cf. *The papal encyclicals*, q.v.) and of
other Vatican officials or departments. This collection, therefore, is of considerable value despite its selectivity and possibly contentious title. The six volumes
are each devoted to a particular topic, and differ somewhat according to the
whims of their editors - some concentrate on more recent pronouncements, while
others range over the whole of Church history. Since the volumes have been
published, at least one update has appeared - for 1979.

109 Catholicism.
Richard P. McBrien.   London: Geoffrey Chapman;
Minneapolis, Minnesota: Winston Press, 1981. 2 vols.

McBrien attempts a non-controversial presentation of the Catholic faith. It
extends beyond the bare documents to a survey of the various positions on the
different doctrines. Each of the volumes contains a useful glossary of theological
terms.

Constitution

110 **The treaty of the Lateran.**
Benedict Williamson.   London: Burns, Oates & Washourne,
1929. 101p.
This book has interest as a contemporary account of the events which led up to
the Lateran Treaty establishing the Vatican City State. The text of the treaty,
and the text of the concordat between the Holy See and the Kingdom of Italy,
are included, as also is the Law of Guarantees, promulgated in 1871, by which
the newly established kingdom unilaterally regulated its position *vis-à-vis* the
Holy See. The author was somewhat sympathetic to fascism, but on the whole
provides an objective account. There are useful quotations on the subject of the
treaty taken from speeches by Pope Pius XI, Mussolini and others.

111 **La Cité du Vatican et la notion d'état.** (The Vatican City
and the idea of a state.)
Dinu Al. Govella.   Paris: Pedone, 1933. 156p. bibliog.
The unique status of the Vatican City aroused a good deal of questioning as to
its juridical position. This is a legal, but not too technical, study of the problem.

112 **The Holy See: its function, form and status in international
law.**
Pio Ciprotti.   *Concilium*, pt. 8 (1970), p. 63-73.
As president of the Vatican City's tribunal, and dean of the Lateran University's
faculty of civil law, Professor Ciprotti is uniquely qualified to distinguish the
various ways the Holy See operates within the framework of international law.
His article is well supplied with references to aid further research, should that be
needed, into a particularly complex area.

113 **The Holy See and international law.**
Horace F. Cumbo.   *International Law Quarterly*, vol. 2
(winter 1948-49), p. 603-20. bibliog.
Cumbo surveys the debate about the international status of the Vatican City. He
discusses the arguments for regarding it as a continuation of the Papal States, but

dismisses them, though Kunz, in an otherwise excellent piece (see below), appears to believe that he agrees with them.

114 **The status of the Holy See in international law.**
Josef L. Kunz. *American Journal of International Law*, vol. 46 (1952), p. 308-14.
Kunz provides a brief and clear exposition of the position of the Holy See - distinguishing it from the Vatican City - in international law. The occasion for the article was a proposal that the US government should send a diplomatic representative to the Holy See. Kunz defends the legal propriety of this (though he says nothing about its political expediency), provided the representative is credited to the Holy See and not to the Vatican City State which, he remarks in passing, is not a sovereign state.

115 **Stato della Città del Vaticano e Santa Sede.** (The Vatican City State and the Holy See.)
Winfried Schulz. *Apollinaris*, vol. 51, pts. 3-4 (1978), p. 661-74.
A serious and well-argued challenge to the generally accepted notion that the Vatican City is a state on a par with other states in international law.

116 **Santa Sede ed organizzazioni internazionali.** (The Holy See and international organizations.)
Bruno Bertagna. *Monitor Ecclesiasticus,* vol. 107 (1982), pt. 1, p. 102-59; pt. 2, p. 284-306; pt. 3, p. 383-428.
According to its mast-head, the *Monitor Ecclesiasticus* has the 'particular approval of the Holy See', and Mgr. Bertagna is on the staff of the Vatican's Secretariat of State. So this article may be regarded as at least a semi-official statement of the Vatican's view of itself and of its role relative to the United Nations, the International Court of Justice, and other similar bodies. This is essentially a legal study.

117 **The Holy See, the Vatican State, and the Churches' common witness: a neglected ecumenical problem.**
Lukas Vischer. *Journal of Ecumenical Studies*, vol. 11, no. 4 (fall 1974), p. 617-36.
In this important but neglected article Dr. Vischer dwells both on the advantages and the problems which arise from the Roman Catholic Church's position in international law because of the Holy See's existence as an independent entity with a voice in international affairs. The author, an official of the World Council of Churches, highlights some of the peculiarities of the Vatican as an independent state.

Legal System

118 **Codex Iuris Canonici.** (The Code of Canon Law.)
Rome: Typis Polyglottis Vaticanis, 1917. 777p.

The legal system governing the Roman Catholic Church is contained in this volume - though in practice it has been in part superseded by individual acts of recent popes. It was first promulgated in 1917, and now exists in innumerable different publications. The one cited here, which has notes by Cardinal Pietro Gasparri, is the basic edition which all others follow. How much of the law contained in the code refers directly to the Vatican City depends on how that term is understood. Book 2, Title 7, chapters 4 ('On the Roman Curia') and 5 ('On legates of the Roman pontiff') clearly do, as also those sections in Book 4 which are concerned with the Roman see's courts and the procedures to be followed therein.

119 **The sacred canons: a concise presentation of the current disciplinary norms of the Church.**
John A. Abbo, Jerome D. Hannah. St. Louis, Missouri; London: B. Herder, 1960. 2nd rev. ed. 2 vols. bibliog.

Only a small part of volume 1 is concerned with the regulations governing the Roman Curia, and the canons in this section are commented upon but not translated. It is, however, a considerable update on the 1917 code.

120 **The canon law digest.**
Edited by James I. O'Connor. Mundelein, Illinois: St. Mary of the Lake Seminary, 1978. 1,289p.

This is the eighth volume in a series which began in 1934 (the first six were published in Milwaukee by the Bruce Publishing Co.), and updates the law of the Church. This particular volume contains, for instance, summaries of regulations affecting the Roman Rota, the Swiss Guard, the conclave, and several other topics directly concerning the Vatican City. There is an excellent index to the mass of new legislation.

121 **Etat actuel des travaux de la commission pontificale pour la révision du Codex Iuris Canonici.** (The progress to date of the work of the pontifical commission for the revision of the Code of Canon Law.)
Wilhelm Onclin. In: *Les droits fondamentaux du Chrétien dans l'Eglise et dans la société.* Edited by Eugenio Corecco, Niklaus Herzog, Angelo Scola. Fribourg, Switzerland: Editions Universitaires; Freiburg, GFR: Herder; Milan, Italy: Giufré, 1980, p. 7-14.

The revision of the law of the Roman Catholic Church which is at present under way will considerably affect the status of the position within that law of the various departments in the Vatican. Professor Onclin's opening address to the 4th International Congress on Canon Law, held in Switzerland in October 1980, is a brief but authoritative outline of the proposed changes.

122 **Juges et avocats des tribunaux de l'Eglise.** (Judges and advocates of the Church courts.)
André Julien. Rome: Catholic Book Agency, 1970. 567p. (Studia et Documenta Iuris Canonici, 1).

Cardinal Julien has produced an exhaustive study of clerical judges and advocates of the Church courts in general, and not just of those operating in the Vatican City, but obviously his remarks apply there *a fortiori*, or so one might think. Neither is the book limited to the matrimonial courts. Some of the book is pietistic, but its third section (p. 225 and following) is devoted to a detailed account of procedure - a procedure wholly different from that followed in courts in the Anglo-Saxon world.

123 **Le contrôle du pouvoir administratif dans l'Eglise.** (The control of administrative authority in the Church.)
Patrick Valdrini. *Pouvoirs*, vol. 17 (1981), p. 75-83.

Juridical control of administrative authority within the Roman Catholic Church dates only from 1967. The establishment of this control is described in the article as 'a small revolution'. Up to that time, administrative decisions called into question had been subjected to examination only by the ecclesiastical superior of the person who had carried out the act in question, and against whom appeal was being made. The new court to cope with this branch of the legal system is part of the Vatican's Signatura Apostolica.

124 **The procedural and administrative reforms of the post-conciliar Church.**
Francis Morrisey. *Concilium*, no. 107 (1977), p. 77-87.

The author briefly surveys the changes in judicial structures within the Vatican, drawing particular attention to the delegation of authority away from the central agencies of the Church.

125 **The function of the Sacred Roman Rota and the Supreme Court of the Apostolic Signatura.**
Zenon Grocholewski. *Concilium*, no. 127, pt. 7 (1979), p. 47-51.

A matter-of-fact summary of the roles played by these two important judicial agencies - the first a court of appeal, the second having the oversight of the fair administration of justice within the Roman Catholic Church as a whole.

126 **Decisiones Seu Sententiae.** (Judgements or opinions.)
Vatican City: Libreria Editrice Vaticana. annual.

Like other courts around the world, the Vatican's marriage tribunal, the Roman Rota, is bound by its own case-law, and therefore publishes a form of 'law reports': a selection of its most notable judgements, or opinions expressed by advocates. These are only produced, however, about a decade after the case was heard (thus the reports for 1972 were published in 1981), and are printed entirely in Latin. False names are used for the parties concerned. The Roman Rota is the final court of appeal in marriage cases, but it is now much less important than it was, since most cases are settled locally. English and American equivalents (in English) of *Decisiones Seu Sententiae* have therefore been made available, though, at least in the case of the English version, not for general circulation.

127 **Power to dissolve.**
John T. Noonan. Cambridge, Massachusetts: Belknap Press, 1972. 489p.

The fundamental study available in English of the workings of the Vatican's marriage courts - which is where the Vatican's legal system touches the lives of ordinary people. Noonan's book covers both the legal and the historical aspects.

128 **Scandal in the assembly.**
Morris West, Robert Francis. London: Pan Books; West Caldwell, New Jersey: Morrow, 1970. 189p.

West and Francis subtitle this 'a bill of complaints and a proposal for reform on the matrimonial laws and tribunals of the Roman Catholic Church', which is a reasonable summary of the content, and an adequate indication of the tone, of their book. The chapter expressly on the Roman Rota is short, informative and pungent.

129 **Marriage annulment in the Catholic Church: a practical guide.**
Ralph Brown. Leigh-on-Sea, England: Kevin Mayhew, 1977. 135p.

The scope of Mgr. Brown's very straightforward account is similar to that of West and Francis cited above. It, too, includes a section on the Rota. The whole tone, however, is much more balanced, not to say judicial, as befits a book by a distinguished Church lawyer.

130 **Leggi e disposizioni usuali dello Stato della Città del Vaticano.** (Laws and regulations governing the Vatican City State.)
Winfried Schulz. Rome: Libreria Editrice della Pontificia Università Lateranense, 1981. 451p. (Utrumque Ius, 7).

This is the first of two volumes - the second is yet to be published - and contains annotated versions of all laws and other regulations formally promulgated which govern the Vatican City State in general. The second volume will contain such regulations as apply to particular Vatican institutions and to its citizens. According to the author's introduction, no other such collection exists. It is arranged chronologically, and is entirely in Italian.

131 **Il diritto di autore nella Città del Vaticano.** (Author's rights in the Vatican City.)
Winfried Schulz. *Apollinaris*, vol. 48, pts. 1-2 (1975), p. 289-300.

It is rare to find legal issues other than those concerning marriage being discussed in the context of the Vatican City. In describing the Vatican's attempts, largely for financial reasons, to claim a form of copyright over certain texts, Schulz highlights the problem of a world-wide church trying to exercise, on a world-wide basis, a law whose validity is strictly speaking restricted to the Vatican City.

Papal Office and Court

132 The papacy as an institution of government in the Middle Ages.
Walter Ullmann. In: *Studies in Church history, II.* Edited by G. J. Cuming. Edinburgh: Nelson, 1965, p. 78-101.
Not as important a work in itself as others by Ullmann cited in this bibliography, but it does help to explain why the mediaeval papacy and its ideology remain so central to the Holy See's ideology today - though, it must be added, that is not the express purpose of Ullmann's piece.

133 Grosseteste and the theory of papal sovereignty.
Brian Tierney. *Journal of Ecclesiastical History,* vol. 6, no. 1 (1955), p. 1-17.
Grosseteste, the 13th-century bishop of Lincoln, is little more than the starting-point for an interesting discussion of the basis of papal authority as it was recognized throughout the Christian world in the Middle Ages, and which forms the basis for its modern claims. Tierney was a pupil of Professor Ullmann, so this, as might be expected, is a heavily legal study.

134 Principles of government and politics in the Middle Ages.
Walter Ullmann. London: Methuen, 1978. 4th ed. 347p.
Only the first part of this book (p. 29-114) deals directly with the papacy and the growth of its authority. Ullmann's approach is now regarded as, perhaps, rather too legalistic, but he has put a stamp on a whole generation of scholarly studies of the mediaeval papacy, and his writings are essential reading.

135 The popes.
Zsolt Aradi. New York: Collier Books, 1962. 128p. bibliog.
The subtitle of this book is 'The history of how they are chosen, elected and crowned'. By now it is somewhat dated in detail, but it still provides a convenient

guide to events surrounding the death of a pope and the election of his successor. The appendixes list, among other items, buildings in Rome which belong to the Holy See but are outside its strict geographical boundaries, and Rome's major ecclesiastical institutions.

136 The triple crown.
Valérie Pirie. London: Sidgwick & Jackson, 1935; Wilmington, North Carolina: Consortium Books, 197[8?]. 346p. bibliog.

The theme of the history of papal elections is an interesting subject, but the approach is disappointingly popular. The period covered is from the election of Calixtus III in 1455 to that of Leo XIII in 1878.

137 Papal elections.
Raimondo Manzini. In: *The Vatican.* Photographed by Fred Mayer. New York: Vendome Press; Dublin: Gill & Macmillan, 1980, p. 183-88.

Manzini - who was once editor of the Vatican's daily newspaper - surveys the history of, and the legislation concerning, the form of election (the 'conclaves') of a pope. Apart from the somewhat pietistic note which enters towards the end, this is an excellent account for anyone looking for quick information.

138 Sede vacante. (The see being vacant.)
Hartwell de la Garde Grissell. Oxford, England; London: James Parker, 1903. 83p.

The title of this short book is the term used officially by the Vatican for the period between the death of one pope and the election of the next. Grissell's account is of the death of Pope Leo XIII and the election and coronation of his successor, Pius X. It has the merit of being something of an insider story, in that it is based upon the diary he kept as a chamberlain of honour to the pope, with numerous ceremonial duties.

139 Acta Apostolicae Sedis. (Acts of the Apostolic See.)
Vatican City: Libreria Editrice Vaticana. 10 per year.

Since 1908 this publication has been the official 'commentary' of the doings of the pope, his officials, and of other official bodies of the Roman Curia. Legislation is promulgated by way of the *Acta*, which comes into force three months from the time of publication. The language used throughout the *Acta* is Latin.

140 Acta Sanctae Sedis. (Acts of the Holy See.)
Rome: Typographia Polyglotta, 1865-1908. 41 vols.

As an annual record of the doings of the Holy See, this publication was a (less official) predecessor of *Acta Apostolicae Sedis*. For its first five years of life it had the considerably longer title of *Acta ex iis decerpta quae apud Sanctam Sedem geruntur in compendium opportune redacta*.

141 The papal encyclicals.
Claudia Carlen. Wilmington, North Carolina: Consortium Books, 1981. 5 vols.

Since 1740 the most important statements made by the popes for general consumption have been contained in letters addressed to the whole Roman Catholic Church, and known as 'encyclicals'. Sister Claudia Carlen has gathered together, or has especially commissioned, translations of all the encyclicals from 1740 to 1981 inclusive, 280 of them in all. There is a useful index in the fifth volume.

142 The Pope Speaks.
Huntington, Indiana: Our Sunday Visitor. quarterly.

This periodical prints the more important papal letters, addresses and other statements of major significance as they appear in the English edition of *L'Osservatore Romano*. There is also a list of all papal utterances appearing in *L'Osservatore* proper. It is, therefore, a fairly good means of keeping up to date with papal pronouncements, but it is selective.

143 The Pope Teaches.
London: Catholic Truth Society. monthly.

This pamphlet-sized publication presents, for the most part, selections rather than full texts from papal sermons and addresses of all sorts, newly translated into English. It has an index, which is particularly helpful.

144 La Documentation Catholique. (Catholic documents.)
Paris: Bayard. fortnightly.

Neither of the above English-language sources for papal and other Vatican pronouncements measure up to the standard of this one. The original language of the text, often of course taken from *L'Osservatore*, is invariably rendered into French, with occasional helpful footnotes and the introduction of cross-headings. But it must be remembered that, although the documents emanating from Rome are given prominence, the periodical is not restricted to these, as the title indicates.

145 Papal heraldry.
Donald Lindsay Galbreath, revised by Geoffrey Briggs. London: Heraldry Today, 1972. 2nd ed. 135p.

The original, 1930, edition of this standard work on papal heraldry presented itself as only the first part of an extensive treatise on ecclesiastical heraldry in general. The remainder was never written, and so the new title is more appropriate for what is probably the most important work on the subject in any language. It is lavishly illustrated with the armorial bearings of the popes, and the last three chapters cover the popes in chronological order. The new edition simply reprints the first edition, and relegates the fair amount of new material to supplementary notes added at the end.

146 A treatise on ecclesiastical heraldry.
John Woodward. Edinburgh, London: W. & A. K. Johnston, 1894. 580p.

As far as papal heraldry is concerned, Woodward's book has certainly been replaced by Galbreath's work (see above). On the other hand Woodward's study is somewhat wider in scope, and the Vatican is, of course, not limited to papal heraldry.

147 Heraldry in the Catholic Church.
Bruno Bernard Heim. Gerrards Cross, England: Van Duren, 1981. 2nd rev. ed. 192p. bibliog.

The author of this well-illustrated book is the pope's representative in London. He is also the Roman Catholic Church's acknowledged expert on heraldry. This treatise is concerned with the history and present practice of, and especially the legal provisions for, ecclesiastical heraldry. Much space is devoted to the papacy and to the Vatican City State, but Archbishop Heim also discusses the rights of those directly in the service of the Holy See to have their own blazons. There is an excellent bibliography.

148 Cardinalis: the history of a canonical concept.
Stephan Kuttner. *Traditio*, vol. 3 (1945), p. 129-214.

Pages 198-214 of this article are highly technical appendixes, and at least half of every page of text is taken up by footnotes, so the body of the article is not as long as it might seem. Furthermore, the subject is rather broader than the title suggests. It is a history of the cardinalate up to the 12th century - and from then on, says Kuttner, there was little change in the concept of cardinal. This is an important study, but seems not to have been given the attention it deserves, particularly in the way in which it explains the origin of the term 'cardinal'. It is not mentioned in van Lierde's little treatise below, for example.

149 What is a cardinal?
P. C. van Lierde, A. Giraud. London: Burns & Oates; New York: Hawthorn Books, 1964. 144p. bibliog.

In theory at least, the cardinals who work in the Roman Curia, the 'Curial cardinals', supply the pope with his chief advisers and the heads of his main departments in the administration of the Church. This brief account of the origins and functions of the cardinalate is a concise survey of a very complicated story. The final four chapters (p. 89-143) discuss the functions of the cardinals in modern times.

150 The papal princes.
Glenn D. Kittler. New York: Funk & Wagnalls, 1960. 369p. bibliog.

An interesting subject popularly, and not too satisfactorily, treated. Most of Kittler's book is a history of the college of cardinals, but the final chapter (p. 340-58) contains a good deal of incidental information about their dress and so on which retains its interest.

151 A papal chamberlain.
Francis Augustus McNutt. London, New York: Longman, Green, 1936. 398p.

Sections of this otherwise tediously self-centred autobiography constitute an interesting insight into life in the papal court from the 1880s to the 1920s.

152 **The ecclesiastical orders of knighthood.**
James Van der Veldt. Washington, DC: Catholic
University of America, 1956. 55p.
Covers, briefly, the history of the major orders of knighthood. The last ten pages
or so describe modern pontifical knighthoods and decorations. This booklet con-
sists of articles from the *American Ecclesiastical Review* for the issues October to
January 1955-56, which may be more readily obtainable than the booklet itself.

153 **The papal forces.**
F. H. Miller. London: Burns, Oates & Washbourne, 1933.
40p.
Concentrates on the Swiss Guard, but includes the Noble Guard, the Palatine
Guard of Honour and the Gendarmes.

154 **The Irish battalion in the papal army of 1860.**
G. F.-H. Berkeley. Dublin: Talbot Press, 1929. 254p.
In 1860 Pius IX appealed for world-wide support from Roman Catholics to
defend the Papal States. Although this book concentrates, as the title indicates,
on the Irish response to that appeal, it contains a sketch of the papal army as
such (p. 26-39) and of the campaign in general. Apart from the very brief
defence of Rome in 1870, this was the last time the papal army went into battle.

Administration

General

155 The growth of papal government in the Middle Ages.
Walter Ullmann. London: Methuen, 1955. 482p.
Professor Ullmann is the acknowledged authority on the theory of papal power in
the Middle Ages. The bulk of this book concerns the development of that theory
from the 7th century to its high point in the 12th. Knowledge of this theory is
essential if one is to understand the relationship between popes and other mediaeval rulers, but it should be stressed that this is not an essay either in political or
in administrative history.

156 Lectures on the history of the papal chancery.
Reginald L. Poole. Cambridge, England: Cambridge
University Press, 1915. 211p.
A learned study of particular interest not only for the early years of the develop-
ment of the papal civil service but also for the organization of Rome itself.

157 The Roman court.
Peter A. Baart. New York: Pustet, 1895. 333p.
Despite its considerable age, still a useful book because of its schematic
representation of the history of the various Congregations, offices and titles within
the Vatican.

158 The Roman Curia as it now exists.
Michael Martin. New York: Benzinger Brothers; London:
R. & T. Washbourne, 1913. 423p.
It is a great pity that there is little or nothing recently published in English to
compare with this, inevitably by now extremely dated, account of the departments
of the Roman Curia. It remains of considerable interest and value to any
historian of the Holy See. A lengthy appendix - over a third of the book - prints

the regulations governing the competence and organization of the various offices of the Holy See as they operated after the reconstruction of 3 November 1908.

159 The Catholic Church in action.
Michael Williams, revised by Zsolt Aradi.   New York: P. J. Kenedy, 1958. 350p. bibliog.

In fact only about half this book (up to p. 170) is of immediate relevance here, and not quite all of that deals, strictly speaking, with the operation of the Vatican. The book was produced on the eve of the second Vatican Council, which changed a good deal, but it remains one of the better, relatively recent and straightforward, accounts of the workings of the Roman Curia in English, though van Lierde's work below is perhaps to be preferred if length is no problem.

160 The Holy See at work.
Peter Canisius van Lierde.   New York: Hawthorn Books, 1962; London: Robert Hale, 1964. 254p. bibliog.

Bishop van Lierde's book is possibly the most satisfactory recent book in English on the organization of the Roman Curia. The author works systematically through the various departments - the Congregations, the tribunals, the commissions and other offices. He has sections on the international Catholic organizations based on the Vatican. There is a very detailed glossary which is not wholly confined to titles and terms used in the Roman Curia, but includes some in more general use within the Catholic Church at large. This is a descriptive work, not a legal study.

161 How the Catholic Church is governed.
Heinrich Scharp.   Edinburgh: Nelson, 1964. 168p.

The title promises rather more than the book delivers, but it still constitutes a useful, brisk survey of the central offices of the Catholic Church, situated in the Vatican. It is out of date on points of detail.

162 The changing Vatican.
Alberto Cavallari.   London: Faber, 1968. 215p.

The particular interest of this book, which is composed of a series of articles and reports originally published in the Milan newspaper *Corriere della Sera*, is the insight which it provides into the way in which, in the mid-1960s, some of the most important functionaries of the papal Curia saw their roles.

163 La Curia Romana: lineamenti storico-giuridico. (The Roman Curia: an historical and juridical outline.)
Nicolò del Re.   Rome: Edizioni di Storia e Letteratura, 1970. 657p. bibliog.

Despite its daunting size, only about half of the book is concerned with the operations of those departments of the Roman Curia which currently exist. The bibliography deserves special mention, as does the index of those papal documents which have legislated for the status and function of the various Congregations, tribunals and so on. This is the standard work on the history and present status of those departments of papal government.

164 **Connaissance du Vatican.** (Understanding the Vatican.)
Paul Poupard. Paris: Beauchesne, 1974. rev. ed. 205p. map.
bibliog.

A better title for Mgr. Poupard's book might have been 'How the Vatican works'.
The author, who has been employed in the Vatican for much of his life, describes
the history and the present status of the Vatican City, but the chief value of this
book lies in its account of the various Roman Congregations, secretariats, tribu-
nals and other offices. Details of how the Vatican City, and the Roman Catholic
Church, are governed will vary from pope to pope, but for an overall view
Poupard's outline of everything from a typical papal day to the number-plates on
Vatican motor cars remains a standard work. There is a useful glossary.

165 **Secretariats and councils of the Roman Curia.**
Giancarlo Zizola. *Concilium*, no. 127, pt. 7 (1979), p.
42-46.

Zizola is a distinguished journalist, and an expert in Vatican affairs. His four-
page survey is highly factual. He gives numbers and budgets, and hints at the
politics of the Curia, especially of the more recently created departments.

166 **The Vatican and its organization.**
Peter Hebblethwaite. In: *The Vatican.* Photographed by
Fred Mayer. New York: Vendome Press; Dublin: Gill &
Macmillan, 1980, p. 15-26.

A very brief introduction to the history of the Vatican but, and rather more
successfully, also a description of the various departments of the Roman Curia
which operate from within the Vatican, set in their historical context.

167 **Serving the communion of Churches.**
Giuseppe Alberigo. *Concilium*, no. 127, pt. 7 (1979), p.
12-33.

Most of Professor Alberigo's article is a very swift survey of the growth of the
authority of the central agencies of the Holy See, located within, or adjacent to,
the Vatican City State. The last few pages, however, are concerned with the
changes which Alberigo would like to see occur in the near future.

168 **Roman 'centrality' - an asset in eastern Europe?**
Hansjakob Stehle. *Concilium*, no. 127, pt. 7 (1979), p.
71-75.

The tendency of the Vatican to draw all authority to itself has been severely
criticized. Stehle defends this 'centralizing' attitude on the part of the Holy See
by pointing out the advantages this has had for the Church in eastern Europe.

169 **La monarchie pontificale et le pouvoir du pape.** (The papal
monarchy and the power of the pope.)
Emile Poulat. *Pouvoirs*, vol. 17 (1981), p. 37-50.

A useful survey, from the pen of a very distinguished Church historian, of the
range, basis and history of papal power in modern times. The article contains an

excellent 'organigramme' which lays out in schematic form the structure of authority in the Vatican.

170 **Les désignations épiscopales dans le droit contemporain.** (The appointment of bishops in contemporary legislation.)
Jean-Louis Harouel. Paris: Presses Universitaires, 1977. 142p. bibliog.

The most obvious and straightforward way in which the Holy See exercises its authority over the world-wide church is through the appointment of bishops. It has almost complete control of this process, a control only occasionally - and decreasingly - limited by political considerations in particular countries. Harouel's book surveys the history of the selection of bishops, and studies especially the ways in which the Holy See gathers information about those of the clergy who are possible candidates for the office. It takes into account the significant changes made in 1971. Not a polemical work, as so many on this subject are.

171 **Papal power.**
Jean-Guy Vaillancourt. Berkeley, California; London: University of California Press, 1980. 361p. bibliog.

According to this book's subtitle, the author has written 'a study of Vatican control over lay Catholic élites', a study, in other words, of how the Vatican exercises its authority. A good deal of the text is padding, the chapters of interest being 3 and 4, section 10 of chapter 5, and chapters 6 and 7. These last two constitute an examination of the relationship between the Vatican and Italian political life from the pontificate of Pius IX (1846-78) to the end of the pontificate of Paul VI in 1978. Although it is somewhat cursory for the earlier period, this examination becomes more detailed as it approaches modern times, and helps to explain the tensions between the Vatican and the Italian Christian Democrat Party. It is a book to be used with caution.

Individual departments

172 **The Sacred Congregation of the Sacraments.**
Robert R. Sheehy. Washington, DC: Catholic University of America Press, 1954. 141p. bibliog. (Catholic University of America Canon Law Studies, no. 333).

The Holy See keeps a strict watch on the 'discipline' of the sacraments and of the other rituals of the Roman Catholic Church. Nowadays it does so through the Congregation for the Sacraments and Divine Worship (pro Sacramentis et Cultu Divino) established in 1975 out of the Congregation of the Sacraments and the Congregation of Sacred Rites. In addition to providing a study of the work of the former of the two organizations, Sheehy usefully outlines the history of the Roman Curia as a whole from 1585 to 1914.

Administration. Individual departments

173 The Sacred Penitentiaria.
William J. Kubelbeck. Somerset, Oregon: Rosary Press, 1918. 124p. bibliog. (Catholic University of America Canon Law Studies, no. 5).

The Sacred Penitentiary goes back to the 13th century, when it had wide powers. It is now restricted to those moral questions affecting individuals which lie outside the sacrament of confession. Its authority was codified in 1935, long after the publication of this discussion of its competence in moral matters, but the new constitution it was then given did not materially change its function.

174 Sacrae Congregationis de Propaganda Fide memoria rerum.
(In honour of the Sacred Congregation for the Propagation of the Faith.)
Edited by J. Metzler. Rome; Freiburg, GFR: Herder, 1971-78. 3 vols. (in 5 parts).

Now renamed, rather less contentiously, the Congregation for the Evangelization of Peoples, the Congregation 'de Propaganda Fide' gave a somewhat sinister word to modern languages. It has been among the most important of the Roman Congregations through which the Holy See governs the Church - in this case the Church's missionary activity. No doubt the Congregation thoroughly deserves these enormous volumes in honour, as its subtitle says in a variety of languages, of '350 years in the service of the missions', but although the articles, also in a variety of languages including English, are of considerable importance for the study of the history of Roman Catholicism as a whole, they say little about the interior workings of the Congregation. Worth knowing about, nonetheless.

175 The Sacred Congregation for the Oriental Church.
Michael W. Dziob. Washington, DC: Catholic University of America Press, 1945. 181p. bibliog. (Catholic University of America Canon Law Studies, no. 214).

The body described in this study of its history and competence has changed its name to the Congregation for Eastern Churches: the plural is highly significant, indicating a growing awareness on the part of the Vatican of the distinctiveness of the eastern Churches which are linked to it. Dziob's study retains an historical interest.

176 La Sacra Congregazione per le Chiese Orientali nel cinquantisimo della fondazione, 1917-67. (The Sacred Congregation for the Eastern Churches on the occasion of the 50th anniversary of its founding.)
Rome: Congregazione per le Chiese Orientali, 1969. 454p.

The Vatican's relations with the eastern Churches which accept papal authority are far from easy, a fact not particularly evident in this somewhat self-congratulatory volume. Nonetheless, in the absence of anything more thorough the book provides a useful survey, and has helpful brief chapters on the individual Churches. The articles, on the history, structure and activity of the Congregation, are for the most part in Italian, though there are some in English and French.

177 **The Sacred Congregation of Seminaries and Universities of Studies.**
James J. Markham. Washington, DC: Catholic University of America Press, 1957. 184p. bibliog. (Catholic University of America Canon Law Studies, no. 384).

The Congregation of Seminaries, regulating the teaching in Catholic universities and, perhaps more importantly, in training colleges for the clergy, had its beginnings in 1588. It took its present form and title of Congregation for Catholic Education (pro Institutione Catholica) as recently as 1967, a decade after the completion of this thesis. Markham's study, however, remains a useful historical and legal survey, and contains helpful lists of colleges directly under the control of the Vatican, both in Rome and elsewhere in the world.

178 **The Congregation of Sacred Rites.**
Frederick Richard McManus. Washington, DC: Catholic University of America Press, 1954. 180p. bibliog. (Catholic University of America Canon Law Studies, no. 258).

For the background to this book, see the note on Sheehy's *Sacred Congregation of the Sacraments* (q.v.). Apart from its concern with ritual, the Congregation of Sacred Rites was responsible for procedures leading to the canonization of saints, which is now undertaken by the Congregation for the Causes of Saints (see the first part of Delooz's book listed below). McManus's somewhat severely legal dissertation considers both aspects of the Vatican's exercise of authority over the Roman Catholic Church.

179 **Sociologie et canonisation.** (Sociology and canonization.)
Pierre Delooz. Liège, France: Faculté de Droit, Université de Liège, 1969. 515p. bibliog. (Collection Scientifique de la Faculté de Droit de l'Université de Liège, 30).

The whole of this study is a fascinating account of who was canonized and why (hence the 'sociology' of the title), and is replete with tables. Interest here, however, is limited to the first part of the volume on 'the selection of saints'. In successive chapters it covers how saints are chosen, the juridical procedure for declaring them saints, the criteria of selection, and those who have been chosen (p. 23-140). This work is now the function of the Congregation for the Causes of Saints, though it was once part of the task of the Congregation of Sacred Rites (see the preceding entry).

180 **The new Inquisition?**
Peter Hebblethwaite. London: Collins, 1980. 173p. bibliog.

The Congregation for the Doctrine (or teaching) of the Faith is the heir to the 'Holy Office', which in turn was the heir to the Roman Inquisition. Like its predecessors it is responsible for the correctness of the Catholic faith as it is taught. In the past it has been one of the most feared of the papacy's departments of state. Peter Hebblethwaite provides a case-study, or rather two case-studies, of the way in which it operates today.

Official publications

181 **Annuarium Statisticum Ecclesiae/Statistical Yearbook of the Church.**
Vatican City: Secretaria Status Rationarium Generale Ecclesiae. annual.

An impressive production, with notes in Latin; English and French, produced by the Vatican's statistical office. Typically it contains detailed tables concerning the territory covered by the Roman Catholic Church, the Church's workforce, educational and welfare institutions, religious orders, Church courts, and the practice of the Catholic religion. The book appears some two years or more after the date to which it refers. It is not, strictly speaking, concerned in particular with the statistics of the Vatican City itself.

182 **Ateismo e Dialogo/Atheism and Dialogue.**
Vatican City: Segretariato Per i Non Credenti. quarterly.

This periodical, with its articles in various languages, is one of the more enterprising of the official and semi-official publications which emanate from the Vatican City. Concerned, as its title indicates, with relations between Roman Catholics and non-believers, it contains articles, book reviews, and an excellent bibliographical section, in addition to the more customary pontifical and other documents or statements.

183 **Bulletin.**
Vatican City: Polyglott Press. 3 per year.

Articles published in several languages by the Secretariat for Non-Christians, though the main languages are English and French. Though dealing in general with relations between Roman Catholicism and non-Christians it seems to concentrate specifically on relations with Islam.

184 **Communicationes.** (Communications.)
Vatican City: Libreria Editrice Vaticana. semi-annual.

The revision of the Church's law is the responsibility of a special pontifical commission which produces *Communicationes*. It is a vehicle for disseminating revised drafts of, and comments upon, changes in the law, as well as of other documents judged to be of relevance, and as such it is essential reading for ecclesiastical lawyers. It is written entirely in Latin. It must be remembered, however, that only a very small part of Church law is directly concerned with the Vatican City.

185 **Information Service.**
Vatican City: Secretariat for Promoting Christian Unity. quarterly.

The secretariat publishes editions in various languages, including English, covering news of relations between Roman Catholic and other Churches.

186 **The Laity Today.**
Vatican City: Consilium pro Laicis. annual.

Of the publications produced by the central offices of the Catholic Church, this is one of the more enterprising. It is published in a variety of languages, and each issue is devoted to one theme thought to be of especial interest to the lay members of the Church.

187 **Notitiae.** (News.)
Vatican City: Libreria Editrice Vaticana. monthly.

Notitiae is produced by the Congregation for the Sacraments and Divine Worship (pro Sacramentis et Cultu Divino) in a variety of languages, but with summaries in French, Spanish, English and German conveniently printed on different coloured papers at the beginning. It carries papal and other official statements or decisions, together with articles from various parts of the world, about Roman Catholic ritual.

188 **Nuntia.** (Announcements.)
Vatican City: Libreria Editrice Vaticana. semi-annual (approx.).

This journal is published by the pontifical commission which oversees the revision of the law for the eastern Churches which are in communion with the bishop of Rome, the Pontificia Commissio Codici Iuris Canonici Orientalis Recognoscendo. It contains papers pertaining to the proposed changes in the law, and other matters concerning its codification. It is a very delicate area for the Vatican, since the eastern Churches are jealous of their relative independence.

189 **Seminarium.** (Seminary.)
Vatican City: Libreria Editrice Vaticana. quarterly.

The articles - on tertiary education in theological colleges and Catholic universities in so far as it is controlled by the Vatican - are printed in a variety of languages, but each is supplied with a Latin summary. The journal is produced by the Congregation for Catholic Education (Congregatio pro Institutione Catholica).

Diplomacy

Theory

190 Vatican diplomacy.

Robert A. Graham. Princeton, New Jersey: Princeton University Press, 1959. 442p. bibliog.

Although this book is recognized as a standard work, it has to be remembered that Fr. Graham is unashamedly an apologist for papal diplomacy. His 'study of Church and state on the international plane' accepts the value of papal diplomacy, and describes the way it has operated in modern times, even while acknowledging some of the criticism which has been made of it. Papal diplomacy implies that, in some sense, the pope is a sovereign, and the author examines the history of this idea. His final section, headed 'Tests and challenges', briefly surveys papal diplomacy during two world wars, the sending of Myron Taylor as President Roosevelt's (and later President Truman's) special representative to the Holy See, and the Holy See's relationship with Soviet Russia.

191 The Holy See and the international order.

Hyginus Eugene Cardinale. Gerrards Cross, England: Colin Smythe, 1976. 557p. bibliog.

The author has himself been in the papal diplomatic service for over thirty years, and it is hardly surprising that this study is largely an apologia for that service. Nonetheless his book is full of information which it is difficult to discover elsewhere, and appendixes include the texts of the Lateran Treaty and of the Vatican City's constituent laws, as well as of various international agreements governing diplomatic and other forms of relations which affect the Holy See. The earlier part distinguishes carefully between what is meant by the 'Holy See' and the Vatican City State. There is an historical survey of diplomacy in general, and of papal diplomacy in particular. This is an essential work of reference.

192 La Sainte-Siège et la diplomatie. (The Holy See and diplomacy.)

Igino Cardinale. Paris: Desclée, 1962. 342p. maps. bibliog.

A systematic study of the theory and practice of papal diplomacy. Very like his other book (see above), but something of a modern classic on the topic of diplomacy within the Church.

193 Natura e funzioni dei legati pontifici nella storia e nel contesto ecclesiologico del Vaticano II. (The nature and function of papal representatives in history and in the ecclesiology of Vatican II.)

Mario Oliveri. Turin, Italy: Marietti, 1979. 320p. bibliog.

More than half, though not a great deal more, of the text deals with papal diplomacy up to 1960. The remainder is concerned with changes since the second Vatican Council. This much-quoted study is heavily legal in its approach. The author, who has since served at the pro-nunciature in London, has produced an abbreviated version (see below) for the Anglo-Saxon world, but no one seriously desirous of understanding papal diplomats' views of their function should neglect this book.

194 The representatives: the real nature and function of papal legates.

Mario Oliveri. Gerrards Cross, England: Colin Smythe, 1980. 192p. bibliog.

A somewhat abbreviated version of Mgr. Oliveri's earlier thesis (see above).

195 The pope's representatives.

Lamberto de Echeverría. *Concilium*, no. 127, pt. 7 (1979), p. 56-63.

A brief, vigorous and far from naïve defence of the role of the papal diplomatic service.

196 The contribution of the Holy See to world peace in the areas of diplomacy, development and ecumenism.

H. E. Cardinale. In: *The Vatican and world peace*. Edited by Francis Sweeney. Gerrards Cross, England: Colin Smythe, 1970, p. 79-121.

As might be expected of an accomplished papal diplomat, Archbishop Cardinale provides a helpful account of papal policy in the areas he mentions in his title during the greater part of the 20th century. Despite its obvious bias in favour of the Holy See, it is a very useful summary.

197 The Church's relations with foreign governments.

Isidoro Martín. *Concilium*, pt. 8 (1970), p. 94-103.

A brief survey of the structures of papal diplomacy, useful if only a short outline is required.

198 **The part played by the Holy See in international organizations.**
Henri de Riedmatten. *Concilium*, pt. 8 (1970), p. 74-93.
The Holy See or, in some instances, the same entity under the alternative title of the Vatican City, has representatives, either in the form of observers or full delegates, in attendance at a score of inter-governmental organizations and a dozen or so non-governmental international bodies. The late Fr. Henri de Riedmatten served as an observer at the United Nations in New York, and on the United Nations' more specialized agencies in Geneva. This article is mainly historical.

199 **Papal diplomacy and the contemporary Church.**
James Hennesey. *Thought,* vol. 46, no. 180 (spring 1971), p. 55-71.
Most, if not all, of the items on papal diplomacy in this bibliography are by apologists for the pope's diplomatic service. Fr. Hennesy's article neatly sums up the views of those who have hesitations about the appropriateness of that service in the modern world.

History

200 **Origines des nonciatures permanentes.** (The beginnings of permanent embassies.)
P. Richard. *Revue d'Histoire Ecclésiastique*, vol. 7 (1906), p. 57-70, 317-38.
This is a seminal, and much referred-to, article about the beginnings of the modern form of papal diplomacy. It is in two parts, as indicated above.

201 **Medieval papal representatives: legates, nuncios and judges-delegate.**
Richard A. Schmutz. *Studia Gratiana*, vol. 15 (1972), p. 443-63.
There is confusion about the origins of papal diplomacy, argues Schmutz, because historians fail to distinguish between the various types of representatives. He neatly describes the function and development of each of the offices he mentions in his title.

202 **Histoire de la représentation diplomatique du Saint Siège des origines à l'aube du XIXᵉ siècle.** (A history of the diplomatic service of the Holy See from its beginnings to the dawn of the 19th century.)
Pierre Blet. Vatican City: Archivio Vaticano, 1982. 537p. bibliog. (Collectanea Archivi Vaticani, 9).
Solidly based upon archival material, this is an excellent history of papal diplomacy and its vicissitudes. It is an historical, rather than a legal, study.

203 **La diplomatie du Saint-Siège après le IIᵉ Concile du Vatican.** (The Holy See's diplomacy since Vatican II.)
André Dupuy. Paris: Téqui, 1980. 343p. 2 maps. bibliog.
Although this is a disappointing book, I know of nothing comparable. Dupuy quickly runs through the usual discussion about Vatican diplomacy in general, and then treats in more detail the peace initiatives taken by Paul VI, the growth of papal diplomacy in Africa, and the so-called 'normalization' of Church-state relations in communist countries, including China. There is next to nothing on Latin America or Great Britain, and not a great deal about the United States. There are a number of very useful statistical tables about the growth, and composition, of the papal diplomatic service.

Treaties

204 **Raccolta di concordati su materie ecclesiastiche tra la Santa Sede e le autorità civili.** (Collection of agreements on ecclesiastical affairs between the Holy See and the civil power.)
Rome: Tipografia Poliglotta Vaticana, 1919. 1,138p.
Though this collection perforce has to omit the all-important concordats the Holy See made with Mussolini's Italy and Hitler's Germany, it gathers together an enormous number of treaties and other forms of agreements between the papacy and a variety of states, ranging from Sicily in 1098 to Serbia in June 1914. The great value of this volume is that the documents are reproduced in the original languages. Unfortunately no translations are appended, except on occasion into Latin.

205 **Church and state through the centuries.**
Sidney Z. Ehler, John B. Morrall. London: Burns & Oates, 1954. 625p.
In some ways this can serve as a translation of the *Raccolta* (see above), though not all the same documents are included. Many of the concordats and other treaties reproduced in this volume are given in full, and the compilers supply a helpful commentary. This book, however, is not limited to Vatican documents. It includes some by local rulers regulating the relationship between Church and state within their own domains.

206 **Concordats et droit international.** (Concordats and
   international law.)
   Henri Wagnon. Gembloux, Belgium: Duculot, 1935. 441p.
   bibliog.

A 'concordat' is the Vatican City's term for what others would call an international treaty. It regulates the relationship between Church and state within the
territory of the government with which it is concluded. Wagnon's book is the
major treatment of the subject. He discusses the Roman Church's international
status, the purpose of concordats, the competent authorities for agreeing to them,
and for ending them, and makes detailed examination of some concordats, though
avoiding those in the news at the time the book was written: the concordats with
Italy and with Germany.

207 **Concordats and international law.**
   Adrianus de Jong. *Concilium*, pt. 8 (1970), p. 104-12.

De Jong's brief article outlines the nature of concordats, and somewhat updates
Wagnon's book. The article concentrates particularly on the problem of marriage
in concordats.

World War II

208 **Actes et documents du Saint Siège relatifs à la Seconde
   Guerre Mondiale.** (Acts and documents of the Holy See
   relative to the Second World War.)
   Vatican City: Libreria Editrice Vaticana, 1965-81. 11 vols.

The editors of these volumes preface the first with a note claiming that the Holy
See was publishing the documents concerning the war because other states (the
United Kingdom, the United States, France, Italy and Germany are mentioned)
had done likewise. That may be so, but it remains, for the Holy See, a highly
unusual publication. It has most often been quarried for information about Pope
Pius XII's attitude to the 'victims of the war' - half the volumes have this as
their subtitle. The series of volumes constitutes a fascinating collection, demon-
strating not only the Holy See's policy but, to some extent, how that policy was
arrived at by the Secretariat of State and how its diplomatic service operates. The
volumes contain speeches by Pius XII, letters exchanged between him and various
civil and ecclesiastical dignitaries, working papers of the Secretariat of State,
correspondence between the secretariat and its representatives abroad, and notes
between the secretariat and diplomats accredited to the Holy See. The documents
are published in their original language.

209 **Records and documents of the Holy See relating to the
   Second World War, I: the Holy See and the war in Europe,
   March 1939-August 1940.**
   Translated by Gerard Noel. London: Herder, 1968. 495p.

This is the English translation of the first volume of the *Actes et documents* (see
above). No more have been published.

210 **The Vatican in the age of the dictators 1922-45.**
   Anthony Rhodes.   London: Hodder & Stoughton, 1973.
   383p. bibliog.
One of the best-documented, most readable general studies readily available of
Vatican policy before and during the Second World War. Rhodes' approach is
sympathetic to the Vatican, though not uncritical.

211 **The Vatican and the war in Europe.**
   Denis Gwynn.   London: Burns, Oates & Washbourne, 1940.
   217p.
A brief essay on papal activity, both personal and diplomatic, to prevent conflict
in Europe, from the election of Pius X to the beginning of the pontificate of Pius
XII. The author is a distinguished historian.

212 **The war and the Vatican.**
   Camille M. Cianfarra.   New York: Dutton, 1944; London:
   Burns, Oates & Washbourne, 1945. 344p.
The author spent seven years in Rome as a correspondent for the *New York
Times*, returning home in 1942. This book is therefore a well-informed, if journal-
istic, account of the Vatican's involvement in events before the Second World
War and in the war's early years.

213 **Vatican diplomacy and the Jews during the holocaust,
   1939-43.**
   John F. Morley.   New York: Ktav Publishing House, 1980.
   327p. bibliog.
Fr. Morley provides a reasonably detached study of a highly controversial episode
in recent papal history. He makes thorough use of the first nine volumes of the
Actes et documents (q.v.) and of other primary sources in order to discuss the
efforts of the Holy See to aid the Jews in Nazi-occupied Europe. The book,
however, has a wider interest. It provides an insight into the operation of the
papal diplomatic service, and into the Holy See's relationship with the warring
powers. As a case-study of the Vatican's intervention in international affairs it is
particularly useful.

214 **Scarlet pimpernel of the Vatican.**
   J. P. Gallagher.   London: Souvenir Press; Toronto: Ryerson
   Press, 1967. 184p.
Somewhat melodramatically told, this is the story of Mgr. Hugh O'Flaherty, an
Irish priest who was working in the Vatican during the Second World War, and
who organized safe houses and escape routes for allied soldiers and airmen. It
recounts a wholly different - and distinctly unofficial - story of the wartime
Vatican from that usually presented.

215 **The Rome escape route.**
   Sam Derry.   London: Harrap, 1960. 239p.
The story of the escape route via the Vatican used during the Second World War
by allied servicemen. Major Derry was one of those whom it benefitted.

Policies

216 The politics of the Vatican.
Peter Nichols.   London: Pall Mall Press; New York:
Praeger, 1968. 373p.

A survey of the Vatican's political history from the earliest times, but concentrating on the period since the death of Pius XII. It is attractively presented with a good deal of atmospheric detail - a journalist's book rather than a scholar's.

217 The eastern politics of the Vatican.
Hansjakob Stehle, translated by Sandra Smith.   Athens,
Ohio: Ohio University Press, 1981. 466p. bibliog.

Stehle's book was first published in German in 1975. This version contains material up to 1979 and so includes the first year of office of a pope from an eastern bloc country. The book is a heavily documented study of the Holy See's diplomatic relations chiefly with the Soviet Union but also with other communist countries since the war. The author was himself in the eastern bloc, working as a journalist, for thirteen years, and was in Rome for ten. Much of what he writes is drawn from his personal experience, as well as from considerable research. It is one of the very best accounts of how and why Vatican diplomacy succeeds or fails. The translation is poor.

218 The Ostpolitik of the Vatican and the Polish pope.
Hansjakob Stehle.   *Religion in Communist Lands*, vol. 8,
no. 1 (Jan. 1980), p. 13-21.

The most recent updating of Stehle's thesis.

219 The Kremlin and the Vatican: Ostpolitik.
Dennis Dunn.   *Religion in Communist Lands*, vol. 4, no. 4
(winter 1976), p. 16-19.

A brief but closely argued statement of Dunn's views on why the Vatican changed its attitude to the communist bloc.

220 The Vatican and communism from 'Divini Redemptoris' to Pope Paul VI.
Paul Higginson.   *New Blackfriars*, vol. 61, no. 719 (April
1980), p. 158-71.

A convenient summary article on the Holy See's political attitudes from the 1937 encyclical condemning communism to 1963. Higginson has something to say on fascism, as well as on communism.

221 **Die Sowjetunion und der Vatikan.** (The Soviet Union and the Vatican.)

Eduard Winter. Berlin, GDR: Akademie Verlag, 1972. 338p.

Winter wrote a three-volume study under the title *Russia and the papacy*, of which this is the third part. It describes the relationship between the USSR and the Holy See from the Russian revolution of 1917 down to 1967. Winter is an East German scholar, and so his views on the relationship between Roman Catholicism and the Soviet Union are rather more sympathetic to the latter than other works listed in this bibliography, with which it may usefully be contrasted.

222 **Entre Rome et Moscou: le Jésuite clandestin.** (Between Rome and Moscow: the secret Jesuit.)

Paul Lesourd. Paris: Lethielleux, 1976. 239p.

As a case-study in the operations of Vatican diplomacy, the story of the 'secret Jesuit', Michel d'Herbigny, is particularly fascinating - and murky. Neither the pope (Pius XI) nor d'Herbigny's religious superiors emerge well from this book.

223 **Rome and Moscow: the bishop who went into the cold.**

B. R. Brinkman. *The Month*, no. 1,326, vol. 239 (March 1978), p. 90-97.

A summary of Lesourd's above study for English readers, with some very pertinent comments upon the Vatican's *modus operandi*.

224 **The Catholic Church and the Soviet government, 1939-49.**

Dennis J. Dunn. Boulder, Colorado: East European Quarterly, 1977. 267p. bibliog.

Professor Dunn does for a decade what Stehle attempts to do for a sixty-year period. He presents a detailed study of the relationship between the Holy See and the USSR. It would, of course, be impossible to discuss the subject adequately without bringing in the other eastern-bloc countries, and Dunn's chapters 9-11 consider in order the Church-state question in Poland, Hungary, and Czechoslovakia during 1948-49, a period of intense persecution. An earlier chapter looks at the period 1944-48 in the same countries. Dunn only reaches the central theme of his book in chapter 4: the opening chapters provide background, both historical and ideological, and are very well worth consulting.

225 **The Vatican and the Kremlin.**

Camille M. Cianfarra. New York: E. P. Dutton, 1950.

Despite its title, the subject of this book is rather broader - the clash in eastern Europe between the Catholic Church and the Communist Party in the second half of the 1940s. Very little of it is directly concerned with Vatican policy, and it is on the whole a somewhat light-weight book. On the other hand it is useful as an easily read survey of the factors which influenced Vatican policy.

226 **The Vatican's east-west policy since Pope John XXIII.**
Robert Graham. In: *The Vatican and world peace.* Edited
by Francis Sweeney. Gerrards Cross, England: Colin
Smythe, 1970, p. 51-78.
Graham is an experienced, if rather partisan, interpreter of Vatican diplomacy.
Despite its title, this article is a fairly brief survey of the shift in papal policy
towards the Soviet Union from Pope John XXIII to the time of its delivery in
March 1968.

227 **Détente and papal-communist relations 1962-1978.**
Dennis J. Dunn. Boulder, Colorado: Westview Press, 1979.
216p. bibliog.
The first chapter of this useful study recounts the history of Catholic-Soviet
relations up to 1962, with an excursus into the times of the tsars. Professor Dunn
follows this with a particularly useful chapter entitled 'Motivation' which considers the reasoning which lay, and to some extent still lies, behind the papal and
the Soviet interest in each other. The remainder of the text looks in turn at the
countries of the Soviet bloc, beginning, naturally enough, with the Soviet Union
itself and ending with Albania, upon which country there are less than two pages.
China is not included.

228 **Lithuania and the Vatican.**
Marite Sapiets. *Religion in Communist Lands*, vol. 4, no. 3
(autumn 1976), p. 4-11.
Useful as a brief study of how one country in the Soviet bloc has been affected
by the Vatican's apparent détente with the Soviet Union.

229 **The Vatican and the silent Church.**
John J. Mowatt. In: *The Ukrainian Catholic Church
1945-75.* Edited by Miroslav Labunka, Leonid Rudnytzky.
Philadelphia: St. Sophia Religious Association, 1976, p.
70-89.
Although the whole of this symposium is intrinsically interesting, the contribution
by Mowatt is of particular significance to users of this bibliography because of
the way it highlights the difficulties experienced by the Vatican in very recent
times to cope on the one hand with the USSR, and on the other with the
nationalist sentiments of a Church in communion with Rome. The author of this
article is most definitely not sympathetic to the Vatican.

230 **La Santa Sede e l'Europa.** (The Holy See and Europe.)
Agostino Casaroli. *Civiltà Cattolica*, vol. 123, no. 2,920
(19 Feb. 1972), p. 367-81.
When he delivered himself of these reflections on the Holy See's policy towards
Europe, Mgr. Casaroli was secretary of the Council for the Public Affairs of the
Church, which was important enough. He is now, however, the cardinal secretary
of state, which makes his speech even more significant.

231 **The emergence of political Catholicism in Italy.**
John N. Moloney. London: Croom Helm; Totowa, New
Jersey: Rowman & Littlefield, 1977. 225p. bibliog.

After the fall of Rome in 1870, Pope Pius IX forbade the involvement of Italian
Catholics in the politics of their newly united country. In 1919 there began, under
Christian inspiration, an Italian 'popular party' (Partito Popolare). Professor
Moloney chronicles the short life of, and the Vatican's attitude towards, the new
party.

232 **The pope and the duce.**
Peter C. Kent. London: Macmillan, 1981. 248p. bibliog.

Although presented as a work on the history of Italy, this study of 'the international impact of the Lateran agreements' dwells at considerable length on the
effect upon Vatican policy of the resolution in 1929 of the 'Roman Question'. It
is concerned in particular with the Vatican's reaction to communism and hence
with the welcome which Pope Pius XI gave to the emergence of Hitler. The book
stops short of the onset of disillusionment with Nazism, but it constitutes an
excellent case-study in papal diplomacy for the half-dozen years it considers in
detail.

233 **Church and state in Italy 1947-57.**
L. C. Webb. Carlton, Australia: Melbourne University
Press, 1958. 60p. (Australian National University Social
Science Monographs, 13).

The Church in Italy, of course, is not to be identified with the Vatican, but in the
period covered by this brief monograph Pope Pius XII was playing an active part
in support of the Italian Christian Democrat Party - not always, it must be said,
in accordance with the wishes of some of the party's leaders.

234 **The Catholic Church and Italian politics: the impact of
secularisation.**
Douglas A. Wertman. In: *Religion in west European
politics*. Edited by Suzanne Berger. London: Frank Cass,
1982, p. 87-107.

Although Wertman's article covers the whole period since the Second World
War, the bulk of it is concerned with the period following the monograph by
Webb cited above. Wertman is in fact chiefly concerned with the impact of
secularization and provides a good deal of data in the form of statistical tables
and analyses. The introductory section, however, is a brisk but very well informed
survey of the effect of Vatican involvement in Italian politics, with excellent
guides to further reading in the notes.

235 **The Catholic Church and Nazi Germany.**
Guenter Lewy. New York: McGraw Hill, 1964. 416p.
map.

Although Lewy concentrates his attention upon the German Catholic bishops,
there is naturally a good deal of information about the Vatican's relations with
the Nazis, and there is a chapter (p. 57-93) on the concordat. There is also a fair
amount of comment upon the Holy See's attitude to Nazism and to totalitarian-

ism in general. It is a thoroughly documented study, not sympathetic to the Church.

236 Anglo-Vatican relations, 1914-1939.
Edited by Thomas E. Hachey. Boston, Massachusetts: G. K. Hall, 1972. 403p.

No major power which had, between the two world wars, diplomats accredited to the Holy See, has so far opened up its official archives to scholars apart from Great Britain. Hachey has simply reproduced the annual reports sent to the Foreign Office by the British ministers to the Holy See, and has provided a brief introduction outlining the history of diplomatic links between London and the Vatican. Clearly, the British minister's chief concern was Anglo-Vatican relations, but the reports throw light on much else, including the Holy See's relations with other countries around the world as they were perceived by a trained observer. They also throw light on the internal workings of the Vatican itself.

237 The United States and the Vatican policies, 1914-18.
Dragan R. Zivojinovic. Boulder, Colorado: Colorado Associated University Press, 1978. 240p. bibliog.

The theme of this book is rather wider than its title perhaps suggests. It is a detailed study of papal peace efforts before, but particularly during and after, the First World War, and of the futile attempt to preserve the Habsburg monarchy. There is an interesting chapter on contemporary American attitudes to diplomatic representation at the Vatican, which is also informative about British attitudes to the same matter.

Economics

238 The Vatican's wealth.
Nino Lo Bello. London: David Bruce & Watson, 1968. 186p.

A not very reliable account of the Vatican's financial structure, written in a journalistic manner and from a distinctly hostile angle. It is of some small historical importance, however, for it forced the Vatican to give a few indications of its investment portfolio.

239 Vatican finances.
Corrado Pallenberg. London: Peter Owen, 1971. 183p.

Pallenberg provides a distinctly more sympathetic account of the state and organization of the Vatican's finances than does Lo Bello above, but this work was written in the light of the information made available after the publication of Lo Bello's book. Also included are a history of papal fund-raising and money-spending. The final chapter details the most recent developments, and foresees further changes.

240 Wordly goods.
James Gollin. New York: Random House, 1971. 531p.

The greater part of this book is concerned with the wealth of the Roman Catholic Church in the United States, and with the people who control the funds. Chapters 17 ('The Vatican: the oldest economy') and 18 ('Vatican finance: myth, reality and performance'), containing some eighty pages between them, are interesting as a critique of Lo Bello's account, but Gollin himself did not fare too well, as events after 1971 were to show.

241 Is the Vatican going broke?
Tana de Zulueta, Franceso d'Andrea. *Sunday Times* (1 June 1980), p. 13.

As the variety of books on the subject bears witness, facts about Vatican finances are particularly difficult to establish. This full-page article by two journalists should, therefore, be treated cautiously. On the other hand the presentation is detailed, clear and informative, and worth consulting if one does not have time to weigh the conflicting accounts in longer treatments of the subject.

242 I francobolli dello Stato della Città del Vaticano, 1929-76.
(Stamps of the Vatican City State, 1929-76.)
Vatican City: Vatican Polyglott Press, 1977. 213p.

One of the main sources of revenue for the Vatican City State is the sale of its many, and highly decorative, series of stamps. This book displays all those produced since the foundation of the Vatican City State in 1929 in a series of excellent colour photographs. Each picture is accompanied by details of interest to philatelists. The sets of stamps are arranged in chronological order, with major divisions for the different pontificates. There is an alphabetic list of issues, though not, unfortunately, of the subjects displayed on the stamps. The information given includes the name of the designer, the date of issue, numbers sold, duration of the sale, and the numbers destroyed at the end of the period. There is also an explanation of the design. The basic text is in Italian, but a translation is provided into a sort of English and inserted into a pocket at the back of the book. The only piece not translated is the 'Presentazione' with which the book opens, in which it is explained that it is not a catalogue in the commercial sense, since no prices are quoted for the items listed. It is simply a piece of thorough documentation on all the stamps which the Vatican City has produced during its lifetime.

Environment

General studies of Rome

243 **La campagna Romana, antica, medioevale e moderna.** (The
Roman campagna in ancient, mediaeval and modern times.)
Giuseppe Tomassetti, updated by Luisa Chinmenti,
Fernando Bilancia. Florence, Italy: Leo S. Olschki,
1979-80. rev. ed. 7 vols. (Arte e Archeologia, 12-18).

The *campagna* is the name given to the territory to the south of the city of
Rome. This enormous work describing it was originally published between 1910
and 1926 in four volumes. In this updated version, the first volume covers the
campagna in general, and the last is a volume of indexes. The remaining volumes
are organized according to the major routes leading out of the city of Rome - the
second volume, for example, deals with the Via Appia, the Via Ardeatina and the
Via Aureliana. The series is of great value for both the history and the topography of the Roman region.

244 **Topografia e urbanistica di Roma.** (Topography and town
planning of Rome.)
Ferdinando Castagnoli, Carlo Cecchelli, Gustavo
Giovannoni, Mario Zocca. Bologna, Italy: Cappelli, 1958.
795p. bibliog.

There are four parts to this massive study: ancient Rome, mediaeval Rome, and
early modern Rome down to 1870 are the first three. The fourth considers Rome
as Italy's capital city from 1870 roughly to the start of the Second World War.
Very thorough.

245 **Rome: profile of a city, 312-1308.**
Richard Krautheimer. Princeton, New Jersey: Princeton
University Press, 1980. 389p. maps. bibliog.

In 312 the 'Edict of Milan' gave official recognition to the Christian religion.
This superb, and superbly illustrated, account of the city of Rome takes the story

of the city from that event down to the beginning of the papacy's temporary exile in Avignon. Krautheimer is at his best when detailing how successive popes expressed through their buildings, and in the decoration of their churches and palaces, their understanding of their role, both spiritual and temporal. But this book is also - and mainly - an excellent account of how the city of Rome grew, declined, and then once more spread out down to the end of the Middle Ages - and, indeed, beyond, for the date 1308 on the title-page is not to strictly adhered to.

246 **The destruction of ancient Rome.**
Rodolfo Lanciani. New York, London: Macmillan, 1907. 279p. bibliog.

A very readable account of what happened to the monuments of Rome from the time of Nero down to the mid-19th century: the effect upon them of the regular invasions of the city, of the city's modernization, and of the use of their materials for the construction of new buildings.

247 **The architecture of Sixtus III.**
Richard Krautheimer. In: *Studies in early Christian, medieval, and Renaissance art.* Richard Krautheimer. New York: New York University Press; London: University of London Press, 1969, p. 181-96.

Sixtus III reigned as pope only from 432 to 440, yet Krautheimer attributes to him considerable importance in the developing style of ecclesiastical architecture in Rome. Krautheimer argues that the buildings associated with Sixtus reflected the papacy's new claim to the cultural and political heritage of pagan Rome. The buildings were, therefore, statements of the prevailing papal ideology. It is a theme which will be met frequently. This version of the article contains Krautheimer's further reflections upon the piece which he originally prepared for publication in 1961.

248 **Architecture in Italy 1400-1600.**
Ludwig H. Heydenreich, Wolfgang Lotz. Harmondsworth, England: Penguin Books, 1974. 432p. bibliog. (Pelican History of Art).

This volume in the Pelican History of Art series covers the period during which Rome was being replanned and beginning to take on its present appearance. The work is so organized that it is relatively simple to turn to sections on the buildings of Rome itself, and on the Vatican.

249 **Studies in Roman quattrocento architecture.**
Torgil Magnuson. Rome: Tipografia del Senato, 1958. 389p. map. bibliog. (Figura 9).

A survey of Rome in the 15th century which retains its value in spite of Westfall's more recent study *In this most perfect paradise* (q.v.) because of the breadth of its scope. It contains a good deal on the topography of Rome before Pope Nicholas V, and a considerable amount of space is devoted to the Roman palaces.

250 **The contribution of Martin V to the rebuilding of Rome.**
R. W. Kennedy. In: *The Renaissance reconsidered: a symposium.* Northampton, Massachusetts: Smith College, 1964, p. 27-52. (Smith College Studies in History, 44).
Martin V's restoration of the Papal States is generally acknowledged (see, for example, Partner's *The Papal State under Martin V*, q.v.), but this side of his activities is less frequently dealt with.

251 **In this most perfect paradise.**
Carroll William Westfall. University Park, Pennsylvania; London: Pennsylvania State University Press, 1974. 228p. bibliog.
Westfall has produced a fascinating, and highly original, study of how Pope Nicholas V, at least in the opinion of Westfall himself, 'invented' modern Rome. His book contains a chapter devoted to the papal palace in the Vatican.

252 **Builders and humanists: the Renaissance popes as patrons of the arts.**
Houston, Texas: University of St. Thomas Arts Department, 1966. 363p.
This book is basically a somewhat elaborate exhibition catalogue, but pages 131-98 provide a useful, well-illustrated survey of the building activities of the popes from 1447 to 1669. The remainder of the book is also of use, being a catalogue of books and manuscripts, a good number of which are of interest for the history of the Vatican, and of the papacy in general.

253 **Painting in Italy 1500-1600.**
S. J. Freedberg. Harmondsworth, England: Penguin Books, 1970. 554p. bibliog. (Pelican History of Art).
Freedberg's book is arranged topographically, so the reader may quickly turn to the pages on the city of Rome which was, of course, at a high point in its history during the century covered by this volume.

254 **Rome of the Renaissance.**
Paolo Portoghesi. London: Phaidon, 1972. 450p. bibliog.
A detailed study of the town planning, and of the architecture, of the city of Rome as begun by Pope Julius II at the opening of the 16th century, and how both progressed for the next fifty years or so.

255 **Art and architecture in Italy, 1600-1750.**
Rudolf Wittkower. Harmondsworth, England; Baltimore, Maryland: Penguin Books, 1958. 428p. bibliog. (Pelican History of Art).
Papal Rome as it now is was largely constructed during the period which Wittkower covers in this volume since he somewhat backdates the beginning of his survey to before 1600. Clearly not all the enormous number of pages (and of illustrations) are concerned with the papal city, but a good many of them are, and for the most part they can be readily distinguished in the table of contents.

Environment. General studies of Rome

The author has nothing on the social history of Rome, and treats only incidentally of the papal court as such.

256 **Roma barocca.** (Baroque Rome.)
Paolo Portoghesi. Rome: Laterza, 1973. 975p. bibliog.

Helpfully divided into two pocket-sized volumes with plenty of pictures, this guide to the architecture of Rome from the 16th to the 18th centuries has a good deal to say about papal views on town planning.

257 **Rome: the biography of its architecture from Bernini to Thorvaldsen.**
Christian Elling. Copenhagen: Gyldendal, 1975. 586p. maps.

Elling provides an exhaustive, if somewhat impressionistic, study of the buildings and of the layout of the city from 1680 to 1797.

258 **L'architettura a Roma al tempo di Pio IX.** (The architecture of Rome in the age of Pius IX.)
Gianfranco Spagnesi. Rome: Multigrafica Editrice, 1978. 94p. bibliog.

Essentially a catalogue of the exhibition mounted to celebrate the centenary of the death of Pope Pius IX, this book contains a useful survey of Roman architecture from 1830 to 1870, and an especially interesting collection of plates illustrating the buildings and the town planning of the city in the 19th century.

259 **Edifices de Rome moderne.** (The buildings of modern Rome.)
Paul Letarouilly. Paris: Morel, 1868. 770p.

An important study since it recalls, in considerable architectural detail (the author was himself an architect), the appearance of Rome at the very end of its time as a papal city. In addition to the 'text' volume listed above, there are three further enormous tomes of drawings. For most practicable purposes, however, the text volume should be sufficient.

260 **Planning the eternal city.**
Robert C. Fried. New Haven, Connecticut; London: Yale University Press, 1973. 346p. bibliog.

Fried's book is concerned with the planning of Rome since the end of the Second World War, though he also provides flashbacks to earlier centuries. It is chiefly of interest as a contrast to the other items mentioned in this bibliography, for it demonstrates how small a part the popes now play in the planning of the city.

261 **Le mure di Roma.** (The walls of Rome.)
Luciana Cassanelli, Gabriella Delfini, Daniela Fonti. Rome: Bulzoni Editore, 1974. 469p. bibliog.

A history of the defences of the city of Rome from ancient Roman times down to 1870.

Individual buildings of Rome

262 **Basilica Vaticana e borghi.** (The Vatican basilica and the
borgo.)
Giulio Tardini. Rome: Istituto Grafico Tiberino, 1936.
114p. bibliog.
Useful now chiefly for its plans and its photographs both of St. Peter's and of
some of the buildings in the immediate neighbourhood.

263 **Castel S. Angelo e borgo tra Roma e papato.** (Castel
San'Angelo and the borgo between Rome and the papacy.)
Cesare d'Onofrio. Rome: Romano Società, 1978. 350p.
bibliog. (Studi e Testi per la Storia della Città di Roma, 1).
For centuries the mausoleum of Hadrian, or the 'Castle of the Holy Angel' as it
came to be known, was the chief fortification of the papacy. D'Onofrio's lively
study tells its story up to the present day.

264 **The history and decoration of the Ponte S. Angelo.**
Mark S. Weil. University Park, Pennsylvania; London:
Pennsylvania State University Press, 1974. 160p. bibliog.
Though no longer obvious to the casual visitor, the Ponte San'Angelo was the
most important bridge across the Tiber as far as the defence of the Vatican was
concerned. Most of this study is devoted to the decoration of the bridge as
undertaken by Bernini.

265 **Rome's historic churches.**
Lilian Gunton. London: George Allen & Unwin, 1969.
191p. map.
Miss Gunton's book is disappointing, but it is a good idea and remains a convenient work of quick reference. She briefly, and systematically, describes the early
churches of Rome, their foundation, purpose and architectural development, and
so on. Many of these churches were closely associated with the papacy, and the
structures of papal authority in the city. It is something of a companion volume
to Stewart's *Roman palaces* (q.v.).

266 **Le Palais de Lateran.** (The Lateran Palace.)
P. Lauer. Paris: Leroux, 1911. 644p. bibliog.
The Lateran Palace served as the papacy's headquarters for longer than the
Vatican has done. This mammoth study traces the history of the building. Over a
third of the book is devoted to documents - ancient descriptions of the Lateran,
inventories and so on. There are many plates.

267 **Restauri e nuove opere nella zona extraterritoriale Lateranse (1961-8).** (Restoration and new construction work at the Vatican's extraterritorial property around the Lateran.)
Armando Schiavo.   Vatican City: Governatorato dello Stato, 1968. 109p. maps.

The Lateran was for a long time the papal headquarters, and it is now one of those properties which, though lying outside the Vatican City proper, belong to the Holy See. This is an account of the work done there by the department of the Holy See responsible for the fabric of the Vatican. It is of interest because of the area it covers, and for its rarity value.

268 **The churches of Rome.**
Roloff Beny, Peter Gunn.   London: Weidenfeld & Nicolson, 1981. 288p. map. bibliog.

The final chapter of this book is devoted to St. Peter's, and there is a useful list of the architects who worked on the new basilica. The whole of the volume, however, is helpful as an introductory guide to the architecture of Christian Rome. It is arranged more or less chronologically, studying the varying styles through the building of churches. It is very well illustrated, though the standard of the photographs - or perhaps of the reproductions -sometimes leaves a good deal to be desired.

269 **Roman palaces.**
H. C. Stewart.   Aberdeen, Scotland: Aberdeen University Press, for the author, 1950. 162p. bibliog.

Brief but neat coverage, in alphabetical order, of Rome's major palaces. This naturally includes the Lateran and the Vatican palaces, but many, if not most, of the others described have papal connections. Informative but summary.

The Vatican

270 **The Vatican and the Basilica of St. Peter, Rome.**
Paul Letarouilly, collated and completed by Alphonse Simil.   London: Alec Tiranti, 1963; New York: Transatlantic, 1966. 3 vols. (in one).

There are brief introductions to the volumes, but otherwise they consist almost entirely of detailed plans and drawings of parts of the Vatican Palace and of the basilica. Indispensible for the architectural history of the Vatican City.

271 **La Vatican sous Paul IV.** (The Vatican under Paul IV.)
René Ancel.   *Revue Bénédictine*, vol. 25 (1908), p. 48-71.

Ancel's 'contribution to the history of the pontifical palace', as he subtitles his article, demonstrates how the works undertaken by Paul IV were doubly unfortunate. In the first place he had destroyed distinguished artistic achievements of earlier times. Secondly, his own additions did not long survive. Most other similar entries in this bibliography are of papal successes - which makes this one different. And of especial interest are the details Dom René supplies of the organization of the work under Paul IV.

272 **I palazzi Vaticani.** (The Vatican palaces.)
Deoclecio Redig de Campos. Bologna, Italy: Capelli, 1967.
287p. bibliog. (Roma Cristiana, vol. 18).
A detailed account, with numerous plans and other illustrations, of the history of the buildings which go to make up the Vatican, apart from the Basilica of St. Peter. The survey is from the 13th to the 19th centuries inclusive.

273 **The apostolic palace.**
Deoclecio Redig de Campos. In: *The Vatican and Christian Rome.* Rome: Libreria Editrice Vaticana, 1975, p. 95-129.
An expertly told architectural history of the papal palace, with some reference also to its decoration.

274 **The art of the Vatican.**
Mary Knight Potter. Boston, Massachusetts: L. C. Page, 1903. 345p. bibliog.
Though undoubtedly old-fashioned, the historical information supplied about the works of art is quite extensive and very useful. The book's subtitle is 'a brief history of the palace and an account of the principal art treasures within its walls'.

275 **The Sistine Chapel before Michelangelo.**
L. D. Ettlinger. Oxford, England: Clarendon Press, 1965. 128p.
This volume is concerned with the 15th-century frescoes in the Sistine Chapel, and their importance in the history of the papacy's understanding of its role in the Church. The book also contains a brief history of the building itself.

276 **Michelangelo: the Sistine Chapel ceiling.**
Charles Seymour. New York: W. W. Norton; London: Thames & Hudson, 1972. 243p. bibliog. (Critical Studies in Art History).
A brief introduction to what is perhaps the world's most famous work of art, together with a collection of relevant documents, and critical comments from a wide variety of authors. There is a very useful bibliography.

277 **Raphael's cartoons in the collection of Her Majesty the Queen and the tapestries for the Sistine Chapel.**
John Shearman. London, New York: Phaidon, 1972. 258p.
Although the cartoons - or some of them - for the tapestries designed by Raphael for the Sistine Chapel belong to the Queen, they are on display in the Victoria and Albert Museum in London, which gives this study a particular interest. Shearman examines the relationship between artist and papal patron, and has

chapters on the commissioning of the work, the significance of the design, and the subsequent history of the tapestries.

278 Frescoes for Pope Julius.
Jean Delumeau. In: *Milestones of history, 4: expanding horizons.* Edited by Neville Williams. London: Reader's Digest; New York: Newsweek, 1974, rev. and expanded ed., p. 138-45.

A brief but illuminating account of the painting of the Sistine Chapel ceiling by Michelangelo, and the subsequent history of the work. Delumeau provides a pagan, as well as a Christian, interpretation of the masterpiece.

279 Vatican stanze: functions and decorations.
John Shearman. London: Oxford University Press, 1972. 58p.

Stanze means rooms or apartments. These are a suite of rooms in the Vatican Palace built for ceremonial use and painted by Raphael and his disciples. Shearman's British Academy lecture (the text also appears in volume 57 of the Proceedings of the British Academy) in effect amounts to a brief history of parts of the Vatican Palace during the early years of the 16th century. More than half the text is taken up by notes.

280 Zur Ikonographie von Raffaels Disputa. (On the iconography of 'The Dispute' by Raphael.)
Heinrich Pfeiffer. Rome: Università Gregoriana Editrice, 1975. 291p. bibliog. (Miscellanea Historiae Pontificiae, 37).

Pfeiffer argues that the frescoes by Raphael in the Stanza della Segnatura reflect the thinking of a particular theologian and, at the same time, display the basis of papal power. It is an important study of the way in which artists were employed to express the ideology of papal authority as it was understood in a particular age.

281 Die Sala di Costantino im Vatikanischen Palast. (The Sala of Constantine inside the Vatican Palace.)
Rolf Quednau. Hildesheim, GFR; New York: Georg Olms, 1979. 1,117p. bibliog. (Studien zur Kunstgeschichte, Band 13).

An exhaustive study of one of the most important series of frescoes in the Vatican Palace.

282 The Casino of Pius IV.
Graham Smith. Princeton, New Jersey; Guildford, England: Princeton University Press, 1977. 125p. bibliog.

The 'Casino' of Pius IV is one of the most distinguished buildings within the Vatican City. It stands in the Vatican Gardens. This well-illustrated study concentrates mainly upon the interior decoration of the Casino, and its significance.

283 **Das Kasino Pius des Vierten.** (The Casino of Pius IV.)
Walter Friedländer. Leipzig, GDR: Hiersemann, 1912.
136p. (Kunstgeschichtliche Forschungen, Band III).
Friedländer's study is rather broader in scope than that above by Graham Smith,
which concentrates on the Casino's interior decoration.

St. Peter's

284 **Saint Peter's.**
James Lees-Milne. London: Hamish Hamilton, 1967. 336p.
bibliog.
A splendidly illustrated history of the basilica - both of the old and of the new -
down to fairly recent times. It includes some trenchant pages on the construction
in 1937 of the Via della Conciliazione.

285 **2000 Jahre Sankt Peter.** (Two thousand years of St.
Peter's.)
Schüller-Piroli. Olten, Switzerland: Summa-Verlag, 1950.
820p. bibliog.
A very detailed history of the Basilica of St. Peter's, with many plans and
illustrations. Recommended for reference purposes, not for general reading.

286 **1506-1606: storia della costruzione del nuovo San Pietro.**
(The history of the building of the new St. Peter's.)
Ennio Francia. Rome: De Luca, 1977. 220p.
An attractively presented and well-illustrated study - detailed but not too techni-
cal.

287 **La Basilica de S. Pietro.** (The Basilica of St. Peter.)
Carlo Galassi Paluzzi. Bologna, Italy: Cappelli, 1975. 532p.
bibliog. (Roma Cristiana, vol. 17).
In addition to the history of both the old and the new St. Peter's, this book
contains studies of some of the church's most notable furnishings and decorations,
and of some of the most important ceremonies to take place there.

288 **The architecture of Michelangelo.**
James S. Ackerman. Harmondsworth, England: Penguin
Books, 1970. 373p. bibliog.
Ackerman's study originally appeared in two separate volumes, the first of text
and plates, the second a catalogue of Michelangelo's work, published in London
by Zwemmer in 1961. The first part of the book contains a short, discursive
account of the design of St. Peter's, while in the second there is a much more
detailed, technical version, together with a couple of pages about Michelangelo's
work on the fortifications of the Vatican.

289 **Treasures of the Vatican.**

Maurizio Calvesi.   London: Sunday Times Publications;
New York: Horizon Magazine, 1962. 207p. bibliog.

This extensively illustrated book provides an outline history of the collections of art in the Vatican, as well as of the buildings themselves. A considerable amount of space is devoted to St. Peter's, both to the buildings and to the decoration of the buildings. Included in the text are accounts of some (never implemented) schemes for reconstruction.

290 **The new St. Peter's.**

Ennio Francia.   In: *The Vatican and Christian Rome.*
Rome: Libreria Editrice Vaticana, 1975, p. 59-93.

The first section of this article is an excellent brief overview of the history of the building of the Basilica of St. Peter's. From p. 80 onwards, however, it simply becomes something of a guide to the interior, and is less useful.

291 **Circle and oval in the square of St. Peter's: Bernini's art of planning.**

Timothy K. Kitao.   New York: New York University Press, 1974. 156p. bibliog.

Within the close confines of the Vatican City State, the best-known view is the sight of St. Peter's Basilica bounded by Bernini's colonnade. Kitao's short study (in effect only seventy-six pages of text) explains how this came about.

292 **Bernini and the crossing of Saint Peter's.**

Irvin Lavin.   New York: New York University Press, 1968. 94p. bibliog.

The immense expanse of the interior of St. Peter's Basilica is dominated by the papal altar. Lavin's monograph describes how, under Bernini's direction, the altar became the focal point.

293 **La cupola di San Pietro.** (The dome of St. Peter's.)

Roberto di Stefano.   Naples, Italy: Edizioni Scientifiche Italiane, 1980. 2nd ed. 111p. bibliog.

One of the most abiding memories of Rome is the dome of St. Peter's. This short study contains a detailed chronology of its construction and restoration.

The master craftsmen

294 **Bramante.**

Arnaldo Bruschi.   London: Thames & Hudson, 1977. 208p. bibliog.

The translator of this volume remarks that Bruschi has written possibly the longest study ever to be published about a single architect. He was asked to abbreviate it for the English version, and produced what was in effect an entirely new monograph. Bramante was the architect first commissioned to design the new Basilica of St. Peter's. He was not, however, long employed upon it, and his designs were later greatly altered by the architects who followed him. Chapter 9 of this book is devoted in the main to the plans for St. Peter's.

295 Michelangelo.
Charles de Tolnay. Princeton, New Jersey: Princeton University Press, 1943-60. 5 vols.

A massive study of the whole of Michaelangelo's life and work, divided up chronologically so that those parts of his life spent in Rome and working in the Vatican can readily be found. The size of the individual volumes is imposing, but the text is not as long as might, at first sight, appear.

296 Michelangelo.
Herbert von Einem. London: Methuen, 1973. 329p.

Outstanding study of the whole of the artist's life and work. The sections on Rome and on the Vatican can readily be isolated from the rest of the text.

297 Raphael.
John Pope-Hennessy. New York: New York University Press; London: Phaidon, 1970. 304p.

The text of this excellent study was originally delivered as a set of lectures. All aspects of Raphael's life and art are covered, including his work in the Vatican.

298 Raphael: a critical catalogue of his pictures, wall-paintings and tapestries.
Luitpold Dussler. London, New York: Phaidon, 1971. 220p. bibliog.

A very helpful, and quick, guide to the whole range of Raphael's work. Each item has notes on provenance, size, location and so on, together with a brief study and bibliography.

299 Gian Lorenzo Bernini.
Rudolf Wittkower. London: Phaidon, 1966. 2nd ed. 286p. bibliog.

A fundamental study by an outstanding scholar, but restricted, for the most part, to Bernini's work as a sculptor. There is, however, a short introductory essay (some thirty pages) on Bernini himself, and a survey of his work in the Vatican.

Education

300 Gli studi dalle prime fonti ai giorni nostri. (Studies from
original sources to our day.)
Mariano da Alatri, Isidoro da Villapadierna. In: *Arte,
scienza e cultura in Roma Cristiana.* Gugielmo Matthiae
and others. Bologna, Italy: Cappelli, 1971, p. 103-97. (Roma
Cristiana, 11).

For those who can manage Italian, this is a particularly useful survey of all the
major teaching establishments, institutes and libraries connected with the Vatican.

301 Storia del Collegio Romano. (The history of the Roman
College.)
Riccardo G. Villoslada. Rome: Gregorian University Press,
1954. 356p. (Analecta Gregoriana, 66).

The Gregorian University is by far the most important of the institutes of higher
education attached to the Holy See, but it began its existence as the Jesuits'
'Roman College'. This excellent, detailed study takes the story of the college from
its foundation in 1551 down to the suppression of the Jesuits in 1773. A brief
final chapter carries the story on to 1824 when control of the Gregorian was
restored to the Society of Jesus.

302 University of the nations.
Philip Caraman. New York: Paulist Press, 1981. 157p.
bibliog.

The subtitle of this work describes it as 'the story of the Gregorian University
with its associated institutes, the Biblical and Oriental, 1551-1962', and the
author's introduction admits that it is 'unashamedly popular history'. There is,
however, no comparable account in any language of what is without doubt the
most important educational institution linked to the Vatican. Fr. Caraman
attaches an 'epilogue' which brings the story down to the present day. The book
is by way of being a panegyric for the 'Greg.', strong on pen-portraits of notable
professors and distinguished alumni, weak on educational method. Indeed little at
all is said of the whole system of Roman clerical education, which has recently
come in for criticism.

303 The Venerable English College Rome.
Michael E. Williams. London: Associated Catholic Publications, 1979. 256p. bibliog.

The 'Venerabile', as the English College is known, can date its origin to 1362 when a group of English merchants bought a house in Rome for the use of their needy countrymen who came to the city as pilgrims. It was not until 1579 that the hospice became a residence for English and Welsh students preparing for priestly work in their home countries. They follow courses at other teaching establishments in Rome - in particular at the Gregorian University. This history covers both style of life and methods of study, and in neither aspect would the English have differed greatly from students in other ecclesiastical institutions in Rome.

304 A history of the Venerable English College, Rome.
A. Gasquet. London, New York: Longman, 1920. 291p.

Cardinal Gasquet's book has been largely superseded by that above by Fr. Michael Williams. It remains, however, a slightly fuller account, treating in greater detail the period down to 1840. The next eighty years are covered in a short concluding chapter.

305 The Beda book: an anthology.
London: Sands, 1957. 300p.

The Beda is one of the two English colleges in Rome training Roman Catholic clergy. The Beda specializes in the education of those who come to the priesthood late. The first twenty or so pages of this collection of pieces from the college magazine are of interest for the history and life of the college, though odd points of interest can be picked up throughout.

306 The Scots College Rome.
London: Sands, 1930. 128p.

The first of the two essays in this brief collection takes the history of the Scots College from its foundation in 1600 down to 1835, the second continues the story on to 1928. A useful history of this 'hall of residence' for Scottish students in Rome, but nothing is said about the educational work of the college. The constitution of 1928 is printed as an appendix.

307 Roman Echoes.
Rome: North American College, 1959. 224p.

A special issue of the North American College's annual publication to celebrate the college's centennial. Several articles are concerned with the history of, and life at, the college both at the end of the 1950s and in the century before.

Literature

The Vatican and the papacy in literature

308 Hadrian the Seventh.
Frederick Rolfe. Harmondsworth, England: Penguin Books, 1982. 360p. (Penguin Modern Classics).

As the title of the series in which it appears indicates, Frederick Rolfe's book, first published in 1904, has established itself as a classic. It is the story of a young priest who wholly unexpectedly becomes the second Englishman (Hadrian IV being the first, hence the title) to be elected pope. He sets about modernizing the Church - the fact that he smokes being particularly significant - but is assassinated. A curiously written, delightful novel, in which Rolfe worked out his own fantasies.

309 Lord of the world.
R. H. Benson. London: Isaac Pitman, 1907. 384p.

The novel is set a century or so after it was written, in a world divided very unevenly between a dominant pagan humanitarianism, led by a man who turns out to be Antichrist, and a remnant of Catholicism centred upon a vast, mediaevalized Rome ruled by Pope John XXIV - though Ireland has also kept faith. Antichrist destroys Rome in what amounts to a bombing raid, and the only surviving, non-treacherous cardinal (an Englishman) flees to Nazareth where he too, now the pope, is betrayed and destroyed. Antichrist triumphs.

310 Dawn of all.
R. H. Benson. London: Hutchinson, 1911. 339p.

Perhaps to redress the balance of *Lord of the world* (see above), Benson sets this novel in an almost entirely Catholic world in the year 1973. The Catholic Church - and hence the pope - rules everywhere except in odd corners such as Berlin and Boston where socialism still lingers. Not for long, however, for the pope turns up at a gathering of socialists in Berlin and threatens to obliterate the lot (again, apparently, in a bombing raid) unless they conform - which they do. The pope then goes on in triumph to England, which by now has been wholly reconciled to the Holy See.

311 **The Vatican cellars.**
André Gide.   Harmondsworth, England: Penguin Books, 1959. 237p.

A heady mixture of Jesuits, Freemasons and shady aristocrats, a plot to kidnap the pope and a fraudulent fund to secure his release. Put on the Index, when there was an Index. Available in many editions.

312 **The representative.**
Rolf Hochhuth.   London: Methuen, 1963. 331p.

Highly controversial, dramatized presentation of the problems of Pius XII and the Jews.

313 **The Jesuit.**
John Gallahue.   London: William Heinemann, 1973. 246p.

A novel loosely based on the intrigues surrounding Michel d'Herbigny (see *Entre Rome et Moscou*, q.v.).

314 **The keys of St. Peter.**
Roger Peyrefitte.   London: Secker & Warburg, 1957. 320p.

The central character of this novel is a young French student priest sent to Rome to serve a worldly and majestic cardinal. After a series of extraordinary adventures involving relics, the Vatican Congregation responsible for the canonization of saints, and the beautiful niece of the cardinal's chaplain, the student returns to his seminary in Versailles a considerably wiser man. This highly entertaining satire of Vatican bureaucracy is a mixture of fact and fiction, but contains enough of the former to arouse the ire of the Vatican, and to bring about the seizure of the novel by the Italian police.

315 **The knights of Malta.**
Roger Peyrefitte.   London: Secker & Warburg, 1960. 287p.

According to George Bull in *Inside the Vatican* (q.v.), only about a quarter of this novel is fictional. It narrates the story of the attempt by the Vatican to effect a complete take-over of the Sovereign Order of the Knights of Malta. The book contains a good deal of factual information about Vatican officials and their intrigues during a period extending from the end of 1949 to the middle of 1956. Among the cast of characters - though both minor ones - figure Mgr. Montini, the future Pope Paul VI, and Mgr. Heim, later to be the papal representative in London.

316 **The agony and the ecstasy.**
Irving Stone.   New York: Doubleday, 1961. 774p. bibliog.

A highly successful evocation of the life of Michelangelo, set against - in part at least - the background of the papal court, also faithfully drawn. Raphael has a walking-on part. Stone includes, unusually for a novel, a glossary of Italian words and phrases, a full bibliography, and a list of the locations of the artist's known works.

Literature. The Vatican and the papacy in literature

317 The shoes of the fisherman.
Morris West.   London: Heinemann, 1963. 302p.

The fisherman of the title is St. Peter. The man who is to step into his shoes is the first Russian to be elected to the papacy. His task: to mediate between Russia and the United States. There is a lot of high-minded discussion about the state of the world and the political significance of papal acts which does not ring true, but this is perhaps West's most popular book to date.

318 Where is the pope?
Gerard Bessiere.   London: Burns & Oates, 1974. 144p.

For once a novel based on the papacy which is not too solemn and portentous (though a little of the latter occasionally creeps in). It is a charming fable of a pope who absconds from the Vatican (one is led to suppose only temporarily) to become a taxi-driver in Paris. It is also amusingly illustrated.

319 The final conclave.
Malachi Martin.   New York: Stein & Day; London: Melbourne House, 1978. 358p.

The first third of this book is a survey of the problems facing Pope Paul VI during his period of office, but especially from 1970 onwards. The remainder is a melodramatic version of what might take place in a conclave to elect Paul VI's successor. It is what *might* take place - it bears no relation to what did in fact happen. It is thoroughly unbelievable, but quite a good story.

320 The vicar of Christ.
Walter F. Murphy.   New York: Macmillan; London: Cassell, 1979. 632p.

The first American pope sets out to transform both the world and the Church. He is assassinated within the year. The United States' answer to *Hadrian the Seventh*? It is not as well written as Rolfe's book, but is a good deal more worldly-wise. There is much on the politics, both secular and ecclesiastical, that surround a pope.

321 The clowns of God.
Morris West.   London: Hodder & Stoughton, 1981. 400p.

A pope has visions of the end of the world, and his worldly-wise cardinals force his abdication. He tells his story to an ex-Jesuit friend, who publicizes it at great risk to himself. The enemy, the incarnation of the powers of darkness, takes the form of an agent of the CIA who comes to an unhappy end, and the ex-pope succeeds in reconciling East and West at least enough for the novel to end on a note of hope for the future.

Recent literary writings by the popes

322 Journal of a soul.
Angelo Giuseppe Roncalli (John XXIII), translated by
Dorothy White. London: Geoffrey Chapman, 1965. 453p.

Basically a spiritual diary, together with other papers of a similar kind, covering the years 1902 to 1963. For someone who achieved such high office, the spirituality he apparently espoused seems almost over-simple. The notes are printed much as he composed them, though in giving permission for their publication after his death he made some small emendations.

323 My bishop: a portrait of Mgr. Giacomo Maria Radini Tedeschi.
Angelo Giuseppe Roncalli (John XXIII). New York:
McGraw Hill; London: Geoffrey Chapman, 1969. 143p.

Mgr. Radini Tedeschi died in August 1914. For the previous nine years Roncalli had served as his secretary, and both his experiences then, and this biography itself, were to have an immense influence on his later career. But as a biography the slant is distinctly devotional rather than socio-historical. Pope John himself said that he wrote it 'for the glory of Holy Church and the edification of the Italian bishops and priests in difficult times'.

324 Mission to France, 1944-1953.
Angelo Giuseppe Roncalli (John XXIII), edited by Don
Loris Capovilla, translated by Dorothy White. London:
Geoffrey Chapman, 1966. 216p.

An accurate, though possibly misleading, title for a collection of sermons, letters and other pieces composed by John XXIII when he was serving as apostolic nuncio in Paris - and therefore dean of the diplomatic corps, a post automatically held by papal nuncios. They range from private letters of condolence to formal addresses presented, on behalf of the diplomatic corps, to successive presidents of France.

325 Pope John XXIII: letters to his family.
Angelo Giuseppe Roncalli (John XXIII), translated by
Dorothy White. London: Geoffrey Chapman, 1969. 833p.

A collection of letters from Roncalli to members of his family ranging from one to his parents after he had arrived in Rome to study for the priesthood, to a long letter to his brother in December 1961 when he was already pope. They display a strong sense of family solidarity which is pleasing, but the rather naïve piety of *Journal of a soul* is often in evidence.

Literature. Recent literary writings by the popes

326 **Illustrissimi: the letters of Pope John Paul I.**
Albino Luciani (John Paul I), translated by Isabel
Quigly. London: Collins, 1979. 286p.

The title is a little misleading since the letters are addressed to characters out of
Dickens, to Pinocchio and so on. They are part literary, part devotional, and were
written for an Italian religious journal when the author was patriarch of Venice,
before his very brief reign as pope. This edition is illustrated with little cartoons
by Papas.

327 **The acting person.**
Karol Wojtyla (John Paul II), translated by Andrzej
Potocki. Dordrecht, Holland; London; Boston,
Massachusetts: D. Reidel, 1979. 367p. (Analecta Husserliana
10).

This is not at all a 'literary' work in the strict sense but 'a contribution to
phenomenological anthropology', to quote the subtitle. It is a philosophical study
of man, of his meaning and purpose. The book is not easy going, especially to the
non-philosophically trained, but it helps to explain not only the pope's theological
writings (which have of course been omitted from this bibliography), but his
poems as well.

328 **The jeweller's shop: a meditation on the sacrament of
matrimony, passing on occasion into a drama.**
Karol Wojtyla (John Paul II), translated by Boleslaw
Taborski. London: Hutchinson, 1980. 63p.

The title is meant to be taken literally: this is a *theatrical* work on marriage, and
as such has been both staged and broadcast. The story concerns three couples
standing outside a shop window choosing rings. Somewhat contrived and distinctly
didactic.

329 **Easter vigil and other poems.**
Karol Wojtyla (John Paul II), translated by Jerzy
Peterkiewicz. London: Hutchinson, 1979. 64p.

Forty-two poems written (under a pseudonym) between 1950 and 1966 when the
author was still a priest and then a bishop in Cracow. The translator, who is
professor of Polish at the University of London, provides a short but very useful
introduction with a note on the distinctly different style of Polish poetry. The
pope's verse is rarely lyrical, and is firmly rooted in the world of work. Curiously,
even the more explicitly religious poems, and these are not many, do not reflect
particularly 'priestly' preoccupations.

330 **Collected poems.**
Karol Wojtyla (John Paul II), translated by Jerzy
Peterkiewicz. London: Hutchinson; New York: Random
House, 1982. 176p.

See the preceding entry for general comment.

Services to Culture and Scholarship

Library and Archives

331 The Vatican museums and library.
D. Redig de Campos.   In: *The Vatican.* Photographed by
Fred Mayer. New York: Vendome Press; Dublin: Gill &
Macmillan, 1980, p. 150-60.

A brief but authoritative survey of the museums and library from the man who
was, until 1979, the director-general of the museums. Redig de Campos's essay
covers both past history and present holdings.

332 La Bibliothèque Vaticane de Sixte IV à Pie XI. (The
Vatican Library from Sixtus IV to Pius XI.)
Jeanne Bignami Odier.   Vatican City: Biblioteca Apostolica
Vaticana, 1973. 477p. bibliog. (Studi e Testi, no. 272).

Though two brief chapters actually carry the history of the Vatican Library back
to 1294, the major part of this splendid piece of research is devoted to the years
from 1471 to 1939. The author's particular interest is the manuscript collection,
for which the Vatican Library is justly famous, but little can be said about this
without including a good deal on the library in general, on its organization, its
staff, its buildings and so on. It must be stressed that this is not a guide to the
manuscript collection, but an account of how the manuscripts were acquired and
conserved.

333 The Apostolic Vatican Library.
José Ruysschaert.   In: *The Vatican and Christian Rome.*
Rome: Libreria Editrice Vaticana, 1975, p. 307-33.

Ruysschaert's piece has very little about the library's holdings, but a good deal
about its architectural and artistic history.

Services to Culture and Scholarship. Library and Archives

334 A service to men of learning.
R. K. Browne. In: *Milestones of history, 4: expanding horizons*. Edited by Neville Williams. London: Reader's Digest; New York: Newsweek, 1974, rev. and expanded ed., p. 59-65.

A useful brief history of the foundation of the Vatican Library, and a description of it as first established. A final paragraph covers the five hundred years since the library's beginnings. The article is imaginatively illustrated.

335 Fifth centenary of the Vatican Library, 1475-1975.
Vatican City: Biblioteca Apostolica Vaticana, 1975. 153p.

This is a catalogue of the exhibition mounted to celebrate the formal foundation of the Vatican Library in 1475. There are sixty-four colour plates displaying items from the exhibition, and lists of some of the library's most interesting and valuable holdings. A useful introduction recounts the history of the collection.

336 Catholicism and history.
Owen Chadwick. Cambridge, England: Cambridge University Press, 1978. 174p. bibliog.

Professor Chadwick's highly entertaining set of lectures is concerned with the gradual opening up of the Vatican's 'secret' archives to scholars in the course of the 19th century. An introductory chapter briefly discusses the history of the archives, but each of the remaining chapters looks at a particular event which, or at a particular archivist who, played a significant part in extending access to the records. As well as providing a fascinating insight into papal attitudes to the challenge presented to the Roman Catholic Church by historical scholarship during the last century, *Catholicism and history* is an outstanding work of historiography in its own right, and very readable.

337 A survey of the Vatican Archives and of its medieval holdings.
Leonard E. Boyle. Toronto: Pontifical Institute of Mediaeval Studies, 1972. 250p. bibliog.

This is a very useful, though, as the title indicates, a chronologically limited, survey of the holdings of the secret archives. A long introduction on the history of the archives is followed by an outline of the different types of holdings, and of what they contain. Indexes and other secondary literature are detailed where they are available. The second part of the book is slightly longer. It is headed 'Notes on selected mediaeval holdings'. There is a general bibliography which lists those documents which have already been printed, as well as works on the archives in general and on particular collections. The bibliography is not easy to use, and ought, perhaps, to be approached by way of the very thorough index. Bibliographical items are asterisked. This is an essential book for anyone contemplating working in the Vatican Archives.

338 Iter Italicum, vol. II. (Italian journey.)
Compiled by Paul Oskar Kristeller. London: Warburg Institute; Leiden, the Netherlands: Brill, 1977. 736p.

The title is misleading. The book is an enormous 'finding list of uncatalogued or incompletely catalogued humanistic manuscripts of the Renaissance in Italian and other libraries'. Pages 310-491 and 581-607 cover the Vatican City itself, but users of this bibliography will find the sections on Rome (p. 89-139 and 560-65) also of value. Although Kristeller restricts himself to 'uncatalogued or incompletely catalogued' manuscripts, his massive work does in effect give substantial guidance to archival holdings in general.

339 **The Vatican Archives.**
Leslie Macfarlane. *Archives*, vol. 4 (1959), no. 21, p. 29-44, no. 22, p. 84-101.
Although not as thorough as the following book by Fish, Macfarlane's excellent little survey has brevity to commend it, together with the fact that it deals explicitly with materials of interest to students of British mediaeval history. Macfarlane outlines the various sections and subsections of the Vatican's archival holdings.

340 **Guide to the materials for American history in Roman and other Italian archives.**
Carl Russell Fish. Washington, DC: Carnegie Institute, 1911. 289p.
Over 200 of the book's pages are concerned with Vatican (and Vatican-related, e.g., those of Congregations) archives. The author stuck closely to his theme of materials for US and Canadian history, but in the process provided a useful guide to the complete collections.

341 **The secret archives of the Vatican.**
Maria Luisa Ambrosini. London: Eyre & Spottiswoode, 1970. 393p. bibliog.
A good deal of incidental information about the Vatican Archives is contained in this book, but it is rather lost amid a mass of historical detail which constitutes little more than a ramble through some of the byways of papal history.

Museums

342 **Art treasures of the Vatican.**
Edited by Deoclecio Redig de Campos. London: Nelson, 1975. 398p.
There are brief accounts of St. Peter's, the Vatican Palace, the library, the archives and so on, but the chief value of this compilation lies in its more than 400 colour photographs of frescoes, books, statues, and many other treasures.

343 Vatican monuments and museums.
Deoclecio Redig de Campos (and others). In: *The Vatican and Christian Rome*. Rome: Libreria Editrice Vaticana, 1975, p. 167-305.

An excellent introductory section-by-section survey (sometimes, apparently, almost show-case-by-show-case) of what is on display in the several different museums within the Vatican. The volume, because of its huge size, is obviously unsuitable as a guidebook, but the various accounts given here could be of considerable benefit to anyone preparing in advance for a visit to one of the world's' richest, and least digestible, collections of treasures.

344 The art treasures of the Vatican.
Bartolomeo Nogara. New York: Tudor Publishing, 1950. 308p.

At the time this book was published, its writer was director-general of the Vatican's museums and galleries. That lends the text a particular authority, but since the text is printed in four languages (of which English is, of course, one) there is not a great deal of it. Still, what there is is informative. The quality of the reproductions is reasonable.

345 Treasures of the Vatican.
Oreste Ferrari. London: Thames & Hudson, 1971. 288p. map.

The first, and somewhat shorter, part of this book is an illustrated history of the popes and art and architecture from the 4th century onwards. The second half is an informed if brief study of some of the more famous works of art in the Vatican, and of the buildings themselves. An excellent introduction.

346 Vatican art.
Karl Ipser. London: W. H. Allen, 1957. 198p.

Pictures of a number of the more important works of art in the Vatican, together with brief captions. There is not much to be said in favour of the reproductions, but the book could be useful as a work of reference.

347 Art treasures of the Vatican Library.
Photographs by Leonard von Matt, text by Georg Daltrop, Adriano Prandi. New York: Harry N. Abrams, 1974. 183p.

The 'museo sacro', established under the authority of the Vatican Library, was founded to further the purpose of religion, and its collection is a major resource for the study of early Christianity. This volume is a collection of splendid pictures of some of the treasures housed in the museum - glass, enamels, ivories and so on - each section being accompanied by an introductory text. Each item displayed in the photographs is briefly catalogued.

Other

348 The choirs.
Giovambattista Salvatori.   In: *The Vatican and Christian Rome*. Rome: Libreria Editrice Vaticana, 1975, p. 355-63.

Very little indeed is available in any language about the musical tradition in the Vatican, despite the fame of its choirs. This piece, on the history of both the Sistine and the rather less well known Julian choirs, is much too short, but is valuable in the absence of anything fuller and readily accessible.

349 The Vatican Observatory.
P. J. Treanor.   Vatican City: Specola Vaticana, 1969. 40p.

The Vatican Observatory was moved out of the Vatican itself to Castel Gandolfo in 1930. This brief descriptive booklet on its particular sphere of activity was written by an English Jesuit who was a member of the observatory staff (the observatory is entrusted to the members of the Society of Jesus).

The Media

350 **The pope and the press.**
Hugh Morley.   Notre Dame, Indiana: Notre Dame
University Press, 1968. 143p.

The pope of the title is Paul VI, and Morley's book is a commentary on what he
said about the media. A useful compilation, but uncritical.

351 **The press and Vatican II.**
Edward L. Heston.   Notre Dame, Indiana; London:
University of Notre Dame Press, 1967. 134p.

Though of limited value, this book, which recounts, for the most part without
comment, how the Holy See handled its relations with the press during the
second Vatican Council, is of interest simply because so little has been written on
this aspect of the Holy See's activities.

352 **L'Osservatore Romano.** (The Roman Observer.)
Vatican City: L'Osservatore Romano. daily.

This newspaper began life as an independent venture by a group of laymen, who
took over an already existing title, and it was bought by the Holy See in 1890.
Strictly speaking it is not an official organ of the Vatican, though it is, and with
reason, minutely studied as such by Vatican commentators. Papal statements and
speeches, declarations by Congregations and so on often appear for the first time
in its pages. Speeches are regularly printed in the language in which they were
delivered, together with an Italian translation. Read with care and with caution it
can be very informative. There is a Sunday edition, with wider appeal and greater
circulation, but that is of less interest for those concerned with Vatican affairs.

353 **L'Osservatore Romano [English edition].**
Vatican City: L'Osservatore Romano. weekly.

This tabloid-sized newspaper contains little or no news as such, but it prints
addresses and other formal statements *in extenso*, and carries a Vatican bulletin
of who did what and who saw whom and for how long on a day-by-day basis. It
is useful, but it is not trusted by expert Vatican-watchers.

354 **The strange case of** *Osservatore Romano.*
Michael J. Walsh. *Month*, no. 1,263, vol. 233 (Nov. 1971), p. 323-26.

A highly critical study of the coverage of news by, and of the style of, the Vatican's daily newspaper.

355 **Vatican Radio between London and Berlin, 1940-1.**
Robert Graham. *Month*, no. 1,303, vol. 237 (April 1976), p. 125-30.

Fr. Graham's interesting article is on the role of the Vatican's radio station at the beginning of the Second World War. It opens with an informative survey of the growth of the station from its foundation in 1931 to 1940.

Reference Works

Encyclopaedias

356 **New Catholic encyclopedia.**
   New York: McGraw Hill, 1967. 15 vols.
Most information about the Vatican City, its various buildings, offices and officers can be found in this encyclopaedia. Entries normally contain bibliographies.
This is the standard reference work in English on Roman Catholicism - and
hence on the Holy See - and can usually be trusted. There are occasional update
volumes.

357 **Enciclopedia cattolica.**
   Vatican City: Ente per l'Enciclopedia, 1949-54. 12 vols.
For anyone who can read Italian, this will probably prove for most purposes a
more satisfactory reference work that the American *New Catholic encyclopedia*
above. Its approach is rather more scholarly (though this is not meant to suggest
that the contributors to the American production are not learned - it is a matter
of approach), and having an Italian bias it has better coverage of matters concerning the papacy and the Vatican City State. The index, however, is difficult to
use.

358 **World Christian encyclopedia.**
   Edited by David B. Barrett.   Nairobi; Oxford, England;
   New York: Oxford University Press, 1982. 1,010p.
The format of this useful compilation forces it to treat the Vatican City (entered
in alphabetical sequence under 'Holy See') as a state on a par with other states,
making projections, for example, about the growth of its population and the
spread of unbelief among its citizens. The piece is short (p. 351-58), but is one of
the best straightforward surveys available. The encyclopaedia is also helpful for
measuring the Vatican's influence world-wide, and for its biographical section.

Serial publications

359 **La Civiltà Cattolica.** (Catholic civilization.)
Rome: Civiltà Cattolica. fortnightly.

Although it is run by the Society of Jesus (and, unlike most other magazines of the society, only Jesuits may write in it), *Civiltà* regularly reflects Vatican attitudes on current issues, political or religious. Its editor is traditionally close to the pope, and the proofs of each issue are read in the Secretariat of State.

360 **Richerche per la Storia Religiosa di Roma.** (Studies into the religious history of Rome.)
Rome: Edizioni di Storia e Letteratura. annual.

This publication only began in 1977, but it is rapidly establishing itself as essential reading for anyone interested in the ecclesiastical life of Rome, and in the way Rome's religious dimension affected the city's inhabitants. Little or nothing directly on the Vatican City has so far (1982) been published, but there is a good deal of background information, including particularly useful guides to archival material.

361 **Miscellanea Historiae Pontificiae.** (A miscellany of papal history.)
Pontificia Università Gregoriana. Rome: Università Gregoriana Editrice. approximately annual.

An important series of monographs published in a variety of languages, occasionally including English. Not all of them are directly concerned with the history and development of the papal Curia, but a great number of them are. In recent years there seems to have been a stress on papal 'foreign relations'.

362 **Päpste und Papsttum.** (Popes and the papacy.)
Stuttgart, GFR: Anton Hiersemann. irregular.

An increasingly important series of studies, often of individual popes, or groups of popes. Recently, however, wider themes affecting the papacy have been treated. The majority of the studies published so far have been in German, but a number have appeared in English.

Directories

363 **Annuario Pontificio.** (The papal yearbook.)
Vatican City: Libreria Editrice Vaticana. annual.

Less than a dozen pages out of some 2,000 contained in this yearbook are concerned with the administration of the Vatican City as such. The greater part of it covers the governance of the Roman Catholic Church both in Rome and world-wide. It lists all bishops, archbishops and cardinals, with brief biographical notes. It details all the many offices of the Roman Curia, and names the members of each department. It has notes on pontifical universities (again in Rome and world-wide), on academies of various sorts, on the papal orders of chivalry, and much else. It also names both the Vatican's own diplomats, with their addresses, and the representatives of countries who maintain some form of diplomatic link with the Holy See. It is an indispensible book for anyone interested in the Vatican from anything more than a simple touristic viewpoint and, despite its size and complexity, its admirable indexes, which take up about a quarter of the book, make it relatively easy to use.

364 **Catholic Almanac.**
Huntington, Indiana: Our Sunday Visitor. annual.
The subtitle of this bulky publication (there are well over 600 pages) is 'The most complete one-volume encyclopaedia of Catholic facts and information on the Church'. That is a fair description, apart from the distinctly North American bias (there are long lists of United States bishops, schools, colleges, Catholic social services and other organizations in the USA, and so on). Most of the more general information is also given an American slant, but it is so enormously detailed that this hardly matters. The chief interest here of the *Catholic Almanac*, however, is that it gives considerable coverage to the Vatican City, most of which is translated from the *Annuario Pontificio*, updated where necessary by the National Catholic News Service. This is a book to be highly recommended to anyone who either cannot lay hands on the *Annuario* or cannot read it.

365 **L'Attività della Santa Sede.** (The activities of the Holy See.)
Vatican City: Tipografia Poliglotta Vaticana. annual.
Two-thirds of the c. 1,000 pages of these volumes chronicle, in the form of a calendar, the doings of the pope during the previous year. The remainder covers, in rather more summary fashion, what each of the Vatican's departments had been doing - and that includes the government of the Vatican City. It is a rather over-long, and too elegantly produced, company report. A useful book for the student of Vatican affairs, however, greatly helped by a detailed analytical index.

Bibliographies

366 **Archivum Historiae Pontificiae.** (Archive for papal history.)
Rome: Libreria Editrice della Pontificia Università Gregoriana. annual.
Appended to the articles and book reviews which constitute the bulk of these massive volumes is a substantial bibliography covering every aspect of the history of the papacy. A good deal of the material included is strictly ecclesiastical and theological, but a number of entries are concerned with papal diplomacy, the Papal States, the city of Rome, Church-state relations and other topics likely to be of interest to a user of this present book. Instructions for consulting the bibliography are given in English, as well as in Latin and French, and the selection of entries is drawn from an enormous range of periodicals, collections of essays, and books. The bibliography is easy to consult, and strongly recommended.

367 A bibliography of the Catholic Church.

London: Mansell; Chicago: American Library Association, 1970. 572p.

The publishers of the American National Union Catalog, pre-1956 imprints, have issued separately in this volume the entries listed by the Library of Congress under the heading 'Catholic Church'. Most of the bibliography, therefore, is taken up with entries under the subheading 'Liturgy and ritual' which lie outside the scope of this bibliography. Some of the others, however, will be of interest. There are, for example, entries for all those departments of the Roman Curia which existed before 1956, including some under the rubric 'Curia' itself. There are entries under popes, treaties, legates and nuncios and so on, though nothing under the Vatican as such. If the researcher knows what he is looking for, then the book could be very useful within the limits indicated, but the lack of a list of subheadings is a distinct disadvantage.

368 The tomb of St. Peter.

Angelus A. De Marco.   Leiden, the Netherlands: Brill, 1964. 261p. (Supplements to Novum Testamentum, 8).

Although only one or two more important publications about the excavations under St. Peter's have been specifically mentioned in this bibliography, an enormous number have appeared. Of these, Fr. De Marco has selected, and for the most part annotated, 870. They are in a variety of languages, but De Marco's abstract of their content is, of course, in English. He first covers the debate about Peter's sojourn in Rome, then deals with the site of the 'Memoria Apostolorum' on the Appian Way, and comes finally to the Vatican excavations themselves.

Index

The index is a single alphabetical sequence of authors (personal and corporate), titles of publications and subjects. Index entries refer both to the main items and to other works mentioned in the notes to each item. Title entries are in italics. Numeration refers to the items as numbered.

J

Jedin, H. 53
Jemolo, A. C. 89
Jesuit 313
Jesuits 222, 301, 349, 359
 periodicals 359
Jeweller's shop: a meditation on the sacrament of matrimony, passing on occasion into a drama 328
Jews of Nazi Europe
 Vatican aid 213
Jews of Nazi Germany
 in literature 312
John, E. 71
John XXIII 13, 90−91, 226
 writings 322−325
John Paul I 94−95
 writings 326
John Paul II 94−98, 218
 writings 327−330
Johnson, P. 97
Jones, P. J. 60
Journal of a soul 322, 325
Judges 122
Judges-delegate 201
Juges et avocats des tribunaux de l'Eglise 122
Julian choir 348
Julien, A. 122
Julius II 82

K

Das Kasino Pius des Vierten 283
Keepers of the keys 68
Kennedy, R. W. 250
Kent, P. C. 232
Keys of St. Peter 314
Kirschbaum, E. 28, 30
Kitao, T. K. 291
Kittler, G. D. 150
Knighthood 152, 363
Knights of Malta 315
Knights of Malta
 in literature 315
Krautheimer, R. 41, 245, 247
Kristeller, P. O. 338
Kubelbeck, W. J. 173
Kunz, J. L. 114
Kuttner, S. 148

L

Labunka, M. 229
Laity, Catholic 186
Laity Today 186
Lanciani, R. 35, 246
Lands of St. Peter 59
Language 101−105
 dictionaries 99
 history 101
 periodicals 100
Lateran Palace 269
 restoration work 266−267
Lateran Treaty 8, 49, 110, 191−192, 232
Latin 101−105
 dictionaries 99
 history 101
 periodicals 100
Latin can be fun 105
Latin for local history 103
Latin: a historical and linguistic handbook 101
Latin: an intensive course 102
Latinitas 100
Lauer, P. 266
Lavin, I. 292
Law 130, 139−140, 163, 191−192
 canon 118−121, 184
 canonization 179
 conclaves 137
 copyright 131
 eastern Churches 188
 marital 9, 12, 126−129, 207
 mediaeval period 75−76
 periodicals 184, 188
Law, International 191−192, 207
 status of the Vatican 111−117, 206
Law of Guarantees 49, 110
Lectures on the history of the papal chancery 156
Lees-Milne, J. 284
Legal system 118−131, 181
Legates 118, 193−195, 201
Leggi e disposizioni usuali dello Stato della Città del Vaticano 130
Leo XIII 138
Lesourd, P. 222
Letarouilly, P. 259, 270
Lewy, G. 235
Lexicon eorum vocabulorum quae difficilius Latine redduntur 99
Libraries 300
Library 7, 331−335, 342

99

75208

Plan of the Vatican City State

The plan opposite shows the more important features.

1   Bronze door – entrance to papal palace
2   Papal palace
3   Loggias
4   Tower of Nicholas V and Vatican Bank
5   Sistine Chapel
6   Borgia Tower
7   Borgia Apartments and Stanze (rooms) of Rapahael
8   Vatican Library and Secret Archives
9   Vatican Library Museum
10 Museums
11 Entrance to museums
12 Art gallery
13 Gate of St. Anna
14 Church of St. Anna
15 Barracks of the Swiss Guard
16 Polyglott Press
17 Offices of *L'Osservatore Romano*
18 Security headquarters
19 Main post office
20 Belvedere Palace
21 Casino of Pius IV
22 Vatican Radio
23 St. John's Tower and the wall of Leo IV
24 Ethiopian Seminary
25 Railway Station
26 Mosaic workshops
27 Government palace – administration of the Vatican City State
28 St. Stephen's Church
29 Palace of the Tribunal
30 Residence of the archpriest
31 St. Charles's Palace
32 St. Marta's Hostel
33 Sacristy and presbytery for St. Peter's
34 St. Peter's Basilica
35 St. Peter's Square
36 Bernini's colonnades

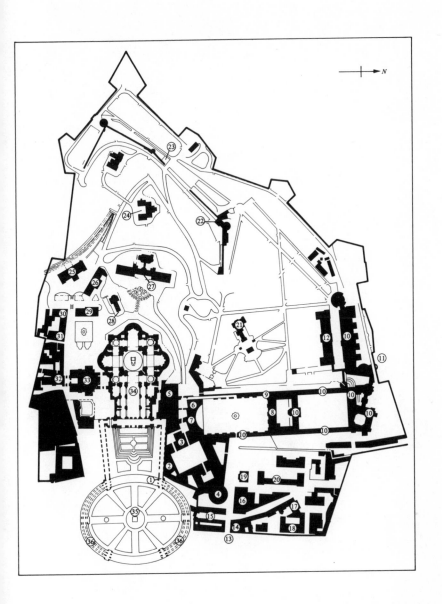

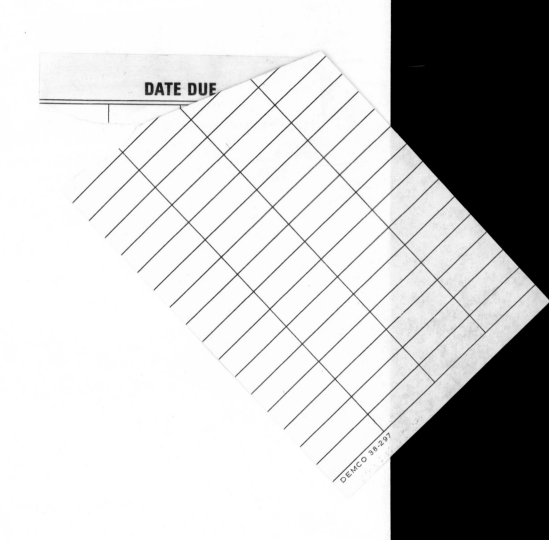

DATE DUE

DEMCO 38-297